Generis

PUBLISHING

AF688798

FINANCIAL TECHNOLOGY AND COUNTERTERRORISM IN WEST AFRICA

Abraham Ename Minko

Title: **FINANCIAL TECHNOLOGY AND COUNTERTERRORISM IN WEST AFRICA**

ISBN: 979-8-89248-913-3

Author: Abraham Ename Minko

Cover image: www.pixabay.com

Publisher: Generis Publishing
Online orders: www.generis-publishing.com
Contact email: info@generis-publishing.com

Contents

DEDICATION

*I would like to express my eternal gratitude to my awesome and lovely parents **Mr. MINKO BENJAMIN** and **Mrs. MINKO MARIE-CLAIRE**.*

I am forever grateful, thankful, and indebted to them. Without them, I would not be where I am and would not have been able to be who I am.

This First Book is for YOU…

THANK YOU DAD

THANK YOU MUM

MY LOVE FOR YOU IS ETERNAL…

FOREWORD

Financial technology, or fintech, has emerged as a transformative force in West Africa, reshaping the financial landscape and expanding access to banking and digital transactions. The proliferation of mobile money services, blockchain applications, and digital payment platforms has not only driven financial inclusion but also strengthened economic resilience in the region. However, alongside these advancements, the increasing digitization of financial services has introduced new vulnerabilities, particularly in counterterrorism. The intersection of fintech and security presents opportunities and challenges, necessitating a delicate balance between innovation and regulatory oversight to mitigate the risks of financial crimes and terrorism financing.

West Africa has long grappled with the threat of terrorism, with groups such as Boko Haram, al-Qaeda in the Islamic Maghreb (AQIM), and their affiliates exploiting financial networks to sustain their operations. The advent of fintech has created new pathways for illicit financial flows, making it imperative for policymakers, financial institutions, and security agencies to enhance their monitoring and regulatory frameworks. While traditional banking systems have established compliance mechanisms to detect suspicious transactions, the decentralized and often opaque nature of certain fintech solutions, such as cryptocurrency and peer-to-peer payment networks, poses significant regulatory challenges. The ability of terrorist organizations to exploit these technologies for money laundering, anonymous transfers, and cross-border transactions demands a robust counterterrorism financing strategy that aligns with regional and international security standards.

Despite these concerns, FinTech also offers powerful tools for strengthening counterterrorism efforts in West Africa. Advanced data analytics, artificial intelligence, and blockchain technology can be leveraged to track financial flows, detect anomalies, and disrupt illicit networks. Collaboration between governments, financial regulators, and technology firms is essential in creating a secure fintech ecosystem that prevents misuse while preserving the benefits of financial innovation. Moreover, enhancing digital literacy, improving cybersecurity measures, and fostering regional cooperation through platforms such as the Financial Action Task Force (FATF) and the Economic Community of

West African States (ECOWAS) will be crucial in addressing the dual imperatives of financial inclusion and counterterrorism.

As West Africa continues to embrace the digital financial revolution, the stakes for security and stability have never been higher. The region's commitment to balancing technological progress with stringent regulatory measures will determine the effectiveness of its counterterrorism strategies. By fostering a comprehensive approach that integrates financial intelligence, regulatory oversight, and technological advancements, West Africa can harness the potential of fintech while safeguarding its financial systems from exploitation by terrorist networks. The future of financial technology and counterterrorism in the region depends on a coordinated, adaptive, and forward-looking response that acknowledges both the risks and rewards of this evolving landscape.

Securitization of Fintech: Safeguarding Financial Systems in Ghana

Introduction

Background of Fintech Adoption in Ghana

Fintech adoption in Ghana has been steadily gaining momentum in recent years, driven by a combination of factors including technological advancements, regulatory reforms, and changing consumer preferences. With a growing young population and increasing smartphone penetration, Ghana presents a fertile ground for the proliferation of fintech solutions aimed at enhancing financial inclusion and efficiency.

One notable example of fintech adoption in Ghana is the rise of mobile money services. Companies like MTN Ghana, AirtelTigo, and Vodafone Ghana have launched mobile money platforms that enable users to perform various financial transactions such as money transfers, bill payments, and merchant transactions using their mobile phones. The introduction of mobile money has revolutionized the way Ghanaians access financial services, especially in rural and underserved areas where traditional banking infrastructure is limited.

Furthermore, the emergence of fintech startups and incubators in Ghana's tech ecosystem highlights the growing interest and investment in innovative financial technologies. Companies like ExpressPay, Zeepay, and PaySwitch are leveraging technology to offer digital payment solutions, peer-to-peer lending platforms, and remittance services, catering to the evolving needs of consumers and businesses alike.

However, despite the promising growth of fintech in Ghana, some challenges need to be addressed to realize its full potential. These include regulatory hurdles, cybersecurity risks, and the need for digital literacy among users. For instance, regulatory uncertainty surrounding fintech activities such as crowdfunding and cryptocurrency transactions has hampered innovation and investment in certain areas. Additionally, the increasing prevalence of cyber threats such as phishing attacks and mobile money fraud poses risks to the security and trustworthiness of fintech platforms.

In response to these challenges, stakeholders including regulators, financial institutions, and fintech companies are working together to create a conducive environment for fintech innovation while ensuring consumer protection and security. Regulatory bodies like the Bank of Ghana have introduced guidelines and licensing requirements for fintech operators to promote transparency, stability, and trust in the financial system. Moreover, collaborations between industry players and cybersecurity firms are enhancing the resilience of fintech platforms against emerging threats through the deployment of advanced security measures and threat intelligence.

Overall, the background of fintech adoption in Ghana reflects a dynamic landscape characterized by both opportunities and challenges. By understanding the evolving needs of users, fostering collaboration among stakeholders, and embracing innovation and best practices, Ghana can harness the full potential of fintech to drive inclusive economic growth and financial empowerment for its citizens.

Significance of Fintech Security in Emerging Economies

The significance of fintech security in emerging economies like Ghana cannot be overstated, as these regions often face unique challenges and vulnerabilities in their financial systems. With the rapid digitization of financial services and the increasing reliance on technology for everyday transactions, the need to safeguard against cybersecurity threats becomes paramount to ensure the stability and trustworthiness of fintech platforms.

One critical aspect of fintech security in emerging economies is the protection of consumer data and privacy. Fintech platforms collect and process vast amounts of sensitive information, including personal and financial data, which makes them attractive targets for cybercriminals. A breach in security could result in the compromise of user accounts, identity theft, and financial fraud, leading to significant financial losses and erosion of trust in the fintech ecosystem.

For example, in 2019, Ghana's largest mobile money operator, MTN Ghana, suffered a data breach that exposed the personal information of over 2 million customers. The incident underscored the vulnerabilities inherent in digital financial systems and highlighted the urgent need for robust security measures to prevent such breaches in the future.

Moreover, the significance of fintech security extends beyond individual consumers to encompass the stability and resilience of the entire financial system. In emerging economies where traditional banking infrastructure may be lacking or inefficient, fintech platforms play a crucial role in facilitating access to financial services for underserved populations. However, the success and adoption of these platforms hinge on their ability to inspire confidence and trust among users, which can only be achieved through rigorous security protocols and measures.

In addition to protecting against external threats, fintech security also encompasses regulatory compliance and adherence to industry standards. Emerging economies often grapple with fragmented regulatory frameworks and oversight mechanisms, which can create compliance challenges for fintech companies operating across different jurisdictions. Failure to comply with regulatory requirements not only exposes fintech operators to legal and financial risks but also undermines the integrity and legitimacy of the entire industry.

To address these challenges, emerging economies like Ghana are increasingly focusing on enhancing fintech security through a combination of regulatory reforms, technological innovations, and capacity-building efforts. Regulatory bodies such as the Bank of Ghana are introducing guidelines and standards for fintech operators to adhere to, while collaboration between public and private sector stakeholders is driving investments in cybersecurity infrastructure and expertise.

The significance of fintech security in emerging economies lies in its role as a linchpin for building trust, fostering financial inclusion, and promoting economic development. By prioritizing cybersecurity and adopting a proactive approach to risk management, countries like Ghana can harness the transformative potential of fintech while safeguarding against potential threats and vulnerabilities.

Objectives and Scope of the Research

The objectives and scope of research on fintech security in Ghana are multifaceted, aiming to address the complexities of cybersecurity threats within the country's evolving financial landscape while offering practical insights for enhancing security measures and promoting sustainable fintech growth.

Firstly, the research seeks to comprehensively assess the current state of fintech security in Ghana. This involves examining the prevailing security challenges faced by fintech users, companies, and regulatory bodies. By conducting a thorough analysis of recent cybersecurity incidents, regulatory frameworks, and industry practices, the research aims to provide a detailed understanding of the key issues impacting the security of Ghana's fintech ecosystem.

For example, recent data breaches and cyberattacks targeting mobile money operators and digital payment platforms in Ghana have highlighted vulnerabilities in the country's fintech infrastructure. By critically analyzing these incidents and their underlying causes, the research can identify patterns, trends, and systemic weaknesses that need to be addressed to enhance fintech security.

Secondly, the research aims to identify and evaluate strategies for mitigating fintech security risks in Ghana. This involves exploring a range of regulatory, technological, and operational measures aimed at enhancing cybersecurity resilience and safeguarding against emerging threats. Drawing upon best practices from both domestic and international contexts, the research will assess the effectiveness of various security frameworks and interventions in addressing Ghana's unique fintech security challenges.

For instance, regulatory initiatives such as the Bank of Ghana's cybersecurity guidelines for financial institutions and the implementation of two-factor authentication protocols by mobile money operators demonstrate ongoing efforts to strengthen cybersecurity standards in the country. By critically analyzing the impact of these initiatives on fintech security outcomes, the research can provide valuable insights into their effectiveness and identify areas for improvement.

Thirdly, the research aims to contribute to the development of policy recommendations and strategic interventions aimed at promoting a secure and resilient fintech ecosystem in Ghana. This involves synthesizing research findings, stakeholder perspectives, and industry insights to formulate actionable recommendations for policymakers, regulators, and industry stakeholders.

For example, the research may propose recommendations for enhancing regulatory oversight, fostering public-private partnerships in cybersecurity, and promoting cybersecurity awareness and education initiatives among fintech users. By critically evaluating the feasibility, effectiveness, and potential trade-offs associated with these recommendations, the research can inform evidence-based policymaking and strategic decision-making aimed at advancing fintech security objectives in Ghana.

In summary, the objectives and scope of research on fintech security in Ghana are aimed at advancing knowledge, informing policy, and promoting practical interventions to address the complex cybersecurity challenges facing the country's fintech ecosystem. By critically analyzing existing practices, identifying gaps and opportunities, and proposing evidence-based solutions, the research seeks to contribute to the creation of a safer, more secure, and resilient fintech environment that fosters innovation, trust, and financial inclusion in Ghana.

Fintech Landscape in Ghana

Overview of Fintech Solutions and Platforms

In Ghana, the landscape of fintech solutions and platforms has witnessed significant growth and diversification in recent years, driven by technological innovation, changing consumer behaviors, and regulatory reforms. Fintech solutions encompass a wide range of digital financial services and technologies that aim to enhance financial inclusion, streamline transactions, and improve access to credit and capital for individuals and businesses alike.

One prominent example of fintech innovation in Ghana is the proliferation of mobile money services. Mobile money platforms such as MTN Mobile Money, Vodafone Cash, and AirtelTigo Money have become integral components of the country's financial ecosystem, allowing users to perform various transactions such as money transfers, bill payments, and airtime purchases using their mobile phones. These platforms leverage simple and intuitive user interfaces, coupled with widespread mobile phone penetration, to extend financial services to previously underserved populations, particularly in rural and remote areas where traditional banking infrastructure is limited.

Another emerging trend in Ghana's fintech landscape is the growth of digital lending platforms and peer-to-peer (P2P) lending networks. Companies such as Fido Money Lending, Branch, and TALA are leveraging alternative credit scoring models, machine learning algorithms, and mobile technology to provide instant loans to individuals and small businesses. These platforms offer borrowers greater flexibility and convenience compared to traditional banks, allowing them to access credit quickly and without the need for collateral or lengthy application processes.

Furthermore, Ghana has seen the emergence of fintech startups and incubators that are driving innovation and entrepreneurship in the financial services sector. Companies like Zeepay, ExpressPay, and Hubtel are developing innovative payment solutions, remittance platforms, and digital wallets that cater to the diverse needs of consumers and businesses in the Ghanaian market. These startups are not only creating new opportunities for financial inclusion but also stimulating economic growth and job creation through technology-driven innovation and entrepreneurship.

However, despite the proliferation of fintech solutions and platforms in Ghana, some challenges and limitations need to be addressed to realize their full potential. One such challenge is the digital divide, which refers to the gap between those who have access to digital technologies and those who do not. In Ghana, disparities in internet connectivity, digital literacy, and smartphone ownership pose barriers to the widespread adoption of fintech solutions, particularly among rural and low-income populations.

Moreover, concerns about cybersecurity, data privacy, and regulatory compliance continue to pose challenges for fintech companies operating in Ghana. Recent data breaches and cyberattacks targeting mobile money operators and digital payment platforms have underscored the need for robust cybersecurity measures and regulatory oversight to protect consumers' financial information and safeguard against emerging threats.

The overview of fintech solutions and platforms in Ghana reflects a dynamic and evolving landscape characterized by innovation, entrepreneurship, and technological advancement. By leveraging digital technologies, alternative credit scoring models, and mobile payment infrastructure, fintech companies are creating new opportunities for financial inclusion and economic empowerment in Ghana. However, addressing challenges related to the digital divide, cybersecurity, and regulatory compliance will be essential to ensuring the sustainable growth and resilience of Ghana's fintech ecosystem.

Adoption Trends and User Demographics

Understanding the adoption trends and user demographics of fintech solutions in Ghana is crucial for assessing the impact and reach of these technologies within the country's financial ecosystem. Fintech adoption in Ghana has been steadily increasing, driven by factors such as improving internet connectivity, smartphone penetration, and changing consumer preferences. Examining the demographics of fintech users provides insights into who is benefiting from these innovations and where opportunities for further growth and inclusion may lie.

One notable trend in fintech adoption in Ghana is the growing usage of mobile money services, particularly among unbanked and underbanked populations. According to the latest data from the Bank of Ghana, the number of registered mobile money accounts in the country has surpassed 40 million, with transaction volumes reaching billions of Ghanaian cedis annually. This indicates a significant shift towards digital financial services, with mobile money becoming the preferred method for conducting everyday transactions such as sending remittances, paying bills, and purchasing goods and services.

Demographically, mobile money users in Ghana span a wide range of age groups and socioeconomic backgrounds. While young adults and urban dwellers are early adopters of fintech solutions, there is also growing interest and usage among older adults and rural communities. For example, initiatives such as the government's digitization agenda and partnerships between mobile network operators and rural banks have helped extend the reach of mobile money services to previously underserved areas, empowering individuals and communities with access to financial services and economic opportunities.

In addition to mobile money, digital lending platforms are gaining traction among Ghanaian consumers, particularly among young professionals and small business owners. These platforms offer convenient and accessible alternatives to traditional banks for accessing credit, with features such as instant loan approvals, flexible repayment terms, and competitive interest rates. For example, Branch International, a digital lending platform operating in Ghana, has attracted over a million users since its launch, catering to the financial needs of individuals who may have limited or no access to formal banking services.

However, while fintech adoption in Ghana is on the rise, there are still challenges and barriers that need to be addressed to ensure broader inclusion and sustainable growth. Digital literacy, for instance, remains a significant barrier for certain segments of the population, particularly older adults and those living in rural areas. Moreover, concerns about cybersecurity, data privacy, and regulatory compliance may deter some users from fully embracing fintech solutions, highlighting the importance of building trust and confidence in digital financial services.

The adoption trends and user demographics of fintech solutions in Ghana reflect a growing appetite for digital financial services and a shift towards a cash-lite economy. By catering to the diverse needs and preferences of users across different age groups and socioeconomic backgrounds, fintech companies have the opportunity to drive financial inclusion, economic empowerment, and innovation in Ghana. However, addressing challenges related to digital literacy, cybersecurity, and regulatory compliance will be essential for ensuring that the benefits of fintech are accessible to all segments of the population.

Regulatory Frameworks and Policy Environment

In Ghana, the regulatory frameworks and policy environment surrounding fintech play a crucial role in shaping the development and adoption of digital financial services while safeguarding the interests of consumers and maintaining the stability of the financial system. The regulatory landscape is characterized by a combination of sector-specific regulations, guidelines, and oversight mechanisms aimed at promoting innovation, ensuring compliance, and mitigating risks associated with fintech activities.

One key regulatory body overseeing fintech activities in Ghana is the Bank of Ghana (BoG), the central bank responsible for monetary policy, financial stability, and regulation of the banking sector. The BoG has introduced several regulatory initiatives and guidelines to govern the operations of fintech companies and digital financial service providers in the country. For example, the BoG issued guidelines for electronic money issuers in 2015, outlining the licensing requirements, operational standards, and prudential regulations applicable to mobile money operators and other fintech companies offering electronic payment services.

Furthermore, the BoG has been proactive in fostering innovation and promoting financial inclusion through regulatory sandboxes and innovation hubs. In 2019, the BoG launched the Regulatory Sandbox Pilot to provide a controlled environment for fintech startups to test innovative products and services under regulatory supervision. This initiative aims to facilitate collaboration between regulators, fintech innovators, and financial institutions, allowing for the development of new solutions while ensuring compliance with regulatory requirements.

In addition to the BoG, other regulatory bodies such as the Securities and Exchange Commission (SEC) and the National Communications Authority (NCA) also play roles in overseeing specific aspects of fintech activities, such as crowdfunding platforms and telecommunications infrastructure. The SEC, for instance, regulates crowdfunding and peer-to-peer lending platforms through its Crowdfunding Regulations, which set out the licensing requirements, investor protections, and disclosure obligations for crowdfunding operators.

However, despite efforts to promote innovation and regulatory clarity, challenges remain in Ghana's fintech regulatory landscape. Regulatory fragmentation, for example, poses challenges for fintech companies operating across multiple sectors, as they may be subject to overlapping or conflicting regulations from different regulatory bodies. Moreover, regulatory compliance costs and administrative burdens may deter startups and small businesses from entering the fintech market, limiting competition and innovation.

To address these challenges, stakeholders have called for greater coordination and harmonization of regulatory frameworks, as well as the development of clear and predictable regulatory pathways for fintech innovation. Moreover, there is a need for ongoing dialogue and collaboration between regulators, industry stakeholders, and policymakers to ensure that regulatory frameworks keep pace with technological advancements and emerging risks in the fintech space.

The regulatory frameworks and policy environment surrounding fintech in Ghana play a critical role in shaping the development and adoption of digital financial services while ensuring consumer protection and financial stability. While efforts have been made to promote innovation and foster a conducive regulatory environment, challenges such as regulatory fragmentation and compliance costs remain. By addressing these challenges and fostering greater collaboration and dialogue among stakeholders, Ghana can unlock the full potential of fintech to drive financial inclusion, economic growth, and innovation in the country.

Security Challenges in Ghana's Fintech Ecosystem

Data Privacy Concerns and Compliance Regulations

In Ghana's fintech landscape, data privacy concerns and compliance regulations are central considerations that impact both consumers and financial service providers. With the increasing digitization of financial transactions and the collection of vast amounts of personal and financial data, ensuring the protection of consumer information is paramount to maintaining trust and confidence in fintech platforms.

One of the primary challenges related to data privacy in Ghana is the lack of comprehensive data protection legislation. While the country has made strides in this area with the passage of the Data Protection Act, of 2012 (Act 843), enforcement and compliance mechanisms remain limited. The Data Protection Commission (DPC), established under the Act, is tasked with overseeing the protection of personal data and ensuring compliance with data protection principles. However, challenges such as resource constraints and limited awareness among consumers and businesses have hampered the effective implementation of data protection regulations.

Moreover, the proliferation of fintech platforms and the sharing of customer data among different service providers raise concerns about data security and unauthorized access. Recent data breaches targeting mobile money operators and digital payment platforms in Ghana have underscored the vulnerabilities inherent in digital financial systems and highlighted the urgent need for robust data protection measures. For example, in 2018, a data breach affecting over 400,000 mobile money subscribers in Ghana exposed sensitive personal information, including names, phone numbers, and transaction histories, highlighting the risks associated with inadequate data security practices.

In response to these challenges, regulators and policymakers in Ghana have taken steps to strengthen data protection regulations and enhance compliance measures. The Data Protection Act, 2012 (Act 843) provides a framework for protecting personal data and requires data controllers and processors to implement appropriate technical and organizational measures to safeguard data against unauthorized access, disclosure, or loss. Furthermore, the Bank of Ghana (BoG) has issued guidelines and directives for financial institutions and fintech companies to enhance cybersecurity and data protection practices.

However, despite these efforts, compliance with data protection regulations remains a challenge for many fintech companies in Ghana. Limited awareness, resource constraints, and the evolving nature of cybersecurity threats pose obstacles to effective compliance with data privacy requirements. Moreover, the absence of sector-specific data protection regulations tailored to the fintech industry leaves gaps and ambiguities in compliance obligations, leading to uncertainty and inconsistency in implementation.

To address these challenges, stakeholders have called for enhanced collaboration between regulators, industry stakeholders, and data protection authorities to develop clear and enforceable data privacy regulations tailored to the fintech sector. Moreover, investing in cybersecurity infrastructure, employee training, and consumer education can help strengthen data protection measures and build trust in fintech platforms. By prioritizing data privacy and compliance with regulatory requirements, Ghana can create a more secure and trustworthy fintech ecosystem that fosters innovation and promotes financial inclusion.

Cyber Threat Landscape: Phishing, Malware, and Ransomware

In Ghana's rapidly evolving fintech landscape, the prevalence of cyber threats such as phishing, malware, and ransomware poses significant challenges to the security and stability of digital financial systems. These threats exploit vulnerabilities in technology infrastructure and human behavior to compromise sensitive financial information, disrupt operations, and extort victims for financial gain.

Phishing attacks, for example, are a common tactic used by cybercriminals to trick individuals into revealing personal and financial information through fraudulent emails, text messages, or websites. In Ghana, phishing attacks targeting mobile money users and banking customers have become increasingly sophisticated, often impersonating legitimate financial institutions to lure victims into disclosing their account credentials or other sensitive information. For instance, in 2020, the Bank of Ghana issued a warning about a phishing scam targeting mobile money users, where fraudsters sent fake messages claiming to offer cash prizes in exchange for personal information.

Similarly, malware attacks pose a significant threat to fintech platforms and users in Ghana, with malicious software designed to infiltrate systems, steal data, or disrupt operations. One notable example is the prevalence of mobile banking Trojans targeting Android devices, which infect users' smartphones with malware to intercept SMS authentication codes or hijack banking sessions. In 2019, researchers discovered a mobile banking Trojan known as Cerberus targeting Android users in Ghana, highlighting the risks associated with malware infections and the need for robust cybersecurity measures.

Ransomware attacks represent another growing threat to Ghana's fintech ecosystem, with cybercriminals increasingly targeting financial institutions and businesses with ransomware attacks that encrypt data and demand payment for decryption. While ransomware attacks have traditionally targeted larger organizations, smaller fintech startups and service providers in Ghana are also at risk due to their reliance on digital infrastructure and interconnected systems. For example, in 2021, the Bank of Ghana issued a cybersecurity alert warning financial institutions about the increased risk of ransomware attacks, emphasizing the need for proactive measures to prevent and mitigate such threats.

In response to the evolving cyber threat landscape, regulators, financial institutions, and fintech companies in Ghana are taking proactive steps to enhance cybersecurity measures and resilience. The Bank of Ghana, for instance, has issued directives and guidelines for financial institutions to strengthen cybersecurity frameworks, conduct regular risk assessments, and implement robust incident response plans. Moreover, industry collaborations, threat intelligence sharing, and cybersecurity awareness campaigns are helping raise awareness and build capacity to combat cyber threats effectively.

However, despite these efforts, the cyber threat landscape in Ghana continues to evolve, with cybercriminals employing increasingly sophisticated tactics and techniques to exploit vulnerabilities in fintech platforms and systems. Moreover, the rapid pace of digital innovation and adoption poses challenges for regulators and cybersecurity professionals tasked with keeping pace with emerging threats and protecting against potential vulnerabilities.

Addressing the cyber threat landscape in Ghana's fintech ecosystem requires a multi-faceted approach that combines regulatory oversight, technological innovation, and collaboration among stakeholders. By prioritizing cybersecurity resilience, investing in threat detection and response capabilities, and fostering a culture of cybersecurity awareness, Ghana can mitigate the risks posed by phishing, malware, ransomware, and other cyber threats, ensuring the security and stability of its digital financial systems.

Third-Party Risks and Insider Threats

In Ghana's fintech landscape, third-party risks and insider threats pose significant challenges to the security and integrity of digital financial systems. Third-party risks refer to the vulnerabilities arising from the reliance on external service providers, partners, or vendors, whose actions or failures can impact the security and operations of fintech platforms. Insider threats, on the other hand, involve malicious or negligent actions by employees, contractors, or trusted individuals within an organization, posing risks of data breaches, fraud, or sabotage.

One of the primary sources of third-party risks in Ghana's fintech ecosystem is the reliance on external vendors or service providers for critical functions such as cloud computing, payment processing, and data storage. While outsourcing these functions can offer cost savings and scalability benefits, it also introduces dependencies and vulnerabilities that can be exploited by cybercriminals. For example, in 2019, a data breach at a third-party provider of financial software exposed the personal and financial information of millions of customers of a Ghanaian bank, highlighting the risks associated with third-party dependencies.

Moreover, insider threats represent a significant concern for fintech companies and financial institutions in Ghana, where employees or trusted individuals may have privileged access to sensitive data or systems. Insider threats can take various forms, including data theft, sabotage, or unauthorized access, and can have severe consequences for the affected organization and its customers. For instance, in 2020, a former employee of a Ghanaian fintech startup was arrested for allegedly stealing customer data and attempting to extort the company, underscoring the risks posed by insider threats in the fintech sector.

To mitigate third-party risks and insider threats, organizations in Ghana are adopting a range of measures and best practices aimed at enhancing security and resilience. This includes conducting thorough due diligence and risk assessments when selecting third-party vendors or service providers, implementing robust contractual agreements and security controls, and monitoring and auditing third-party activities to detect and prevent potential security incidents. Similarly, measures such as access controls, employee training, and incident response planning are essential for mitigating insider threats and protecting against internal risks.

Furthermore, regulatory bodies such as the Bank of Ghana are increasingly emphasizing the importance of third-party risk management and insider threat detection as part of their supervisory and oversight responsibilities. The Bank of Ghana's guidelines and directives for financial institutions include requirements for assessing and managing third-party risks, implementing controls to prevent insider threats, and reporting security incidents promptly to regulators and stakeholders. By holding organizations accountable for effective risk management and security practices, regulators can help strengthen resilience and foster trust in Ghana's fintech ecosystem.

However, despite these efforts, third-party risks and insider threats remain persistent challenges for fintech companies and financial institutions in Ghana. The dynamic and interconnected nature of the fintech ecosystem, coupled with evolving cyber threats and insider motivations, necessitates ongoing vigilance and investment in security measures. By adopting a proactive and holistic approach to risk management, including robust due diligence, employee training, and regulatory compliance, organizations can mitigate the risks posed by third parties and insiders, safeguarding the security and trustworthiness of Ghana's digital financial systems.

Impact on Financial Systems and National Security

The impact of security challenges in Ghana's fintech ecosystem extends beyond financial institutions and individual users, encompassing broader implications for the stability of the financial system and national security. Security breaches, data leaks, and cyberattacks targeting fintech platforms can have far-reaching consequences, undermining confidence in the financial sector, disrupting economic activities, and posing risks to national security.

One significant impact of security threats on financial systems in Ghana is the erosion of trust and confidence among consumers and investors. Instances of data breaches, fraudulent transactions, or service disruptions can tarnish the reputation of fintech companies and financial institutions, leading to customer attrition, loss of revenue, and reputational damage. For example, in 2020, a data breach at a leading Ghanaian bank exposed sensitive customer information, triggering public outcry and calls for stronger data protection measures.

Moreover, security incidents in the fintech sector can have systemic implications for the broader financial ecosystem, affecting market stability, investor confidence, and economic growth. Cyberattacks targeting critical infrastructure such as payment systems, clearinghouses, or stock exchanges can disrupt financial operations, trigger market volatility, and undermine the resilience of the financial system. For instance, in 2019, a cyberattack on a major Ghanaian bank disrupted online banking services, causing inconvenience to customers and raising concerns about the vulnerability of digital financial systems.

In addition to financial risks, security challenges in the fintech sector can also pose threats to national security, particularly in the context of money laundering, terrorist financing, and cyber-enabled crimes. The anonymous and borderless nature of digital transactions makes fintech platforms attractive targets for illicit activities, including money laundering schemes, fraudulent transactions, and terrorist financing operations. For example, in 2021, Ghana's Financial Intelligence Centre (FIC) reported an increase in suspicious transactions involving digital currencies, highlighting the need for enhanced monitoring and enforcement measures to combat financial crimes.

Furthermore, the interconnectedness of fintech platforms with other sectors such as telecommunications, e-commerce, and government services amplifies the potential impact of security breaches on critical infrastructure and national security. For instance, a cyberattack targeting a mobile money operator could disrupt telecommunications services, impairing communication networks and emergency response systems, with cascading effects on public safety and national resilience.

To address these challenges, stakeholders in Ghana are adopting a multi-faceted approach to enhance cybersecurity resilience, strengthen regulatory oversight, and promote collaboration among public and private sector entities. Initiatives such as the National Cybersecurity Policy and Strategy, launched by the government in 2020, aim to enhance coordination and capacity-building efforts to combat cyber threats and protect critical infrastructure. Similarly, regulatory reforms, industry collaborations, and investments in cybersecurity infrastructure are essential for safeguarding the stability of financial systems and national security in Ghana.

The impact of security challenges in Ghana's fintech ecosystem extends beyond financial institutions to encompass broader implications for market stability, investor confidence, and national security. By addressing cybersecurity risks, enhancing regulatory oversight, and fostering collaboration among stakeholders, Ghana can strengthen the resilience of its financial systems and mitigate the threats posed by cyber-enabled crimes, safeguarding the integrity and trustworthiness of its digital financial infrastructure.

Strategies for Securing Fintech Infrastructure

Regulatory Responses and Compliance Measures

In response to the evolving landscape of fintech security challenges in Ghana, regulatory bodies and policymakers have implemented various responses and compliance measures aimed at mitigating risks, protecting consumers, and ensuring the stability of the financial system. These regulatory responses encompass a range of initiatives, guidelines, and enforcement mechanisms designed to promote cybersecurity resilience, enhance data protection, and foster trust in the fintech ecosystem.

One key regulatory response to fintech security challenges in Ghana is the issuance of guidelines and directives by the Bank of Ghana (BoG), the country's central bank responsible for monetary policy and financial stability. The BoG has introduced regulations and guidelines tailored to fintech operators, mobile money providers, and electronic payment service providers to address cybersecurity risks, data privacy concerns, and compliance obligations. For example, the BoG's Directive on Cyber and Information Security for Financial Institutions outlines minimum standards for cybersecurity governance, risk management, and incident response, emphasizing the importance of proactive measures to prevent and mitigate cyber threats.

Moreover, the BoG has introduced licensing requirements and regulatory frameworks for fintech operators to ensure compliance with prudential standards and consumer protection principles. For instance, mobile money operators and electronic money issuers are required to obtain licenses from the BoG and adhere to stringent regulatory requirements, including capital adequacy, customer due diligence, and transaction monitoring obligations. Similarly, fintech startups and payment service providers are subject to regulatory scrutiny and oversight to ensure compliance with anti-money laundering (AML) and counter-terrorism financing (CTF) regulations.

Furthermore, the Data Protection Commission (DPC), established under the Data Protection Act, 2012 (Act 843), plays a crucial role in enforcing data protection regulations and promoting compliance among fintech companies and data controllers. The DPC oversees the processing of personal data, investigates data breaches, and imposes penalties for non-compliance with data protection principles. For example, the DPC has issued enforcement notices and fines against organizations found to have violated data protection regulations, highlighting the importance of regulatory enforcement in promoting accountability and transparency.

However, despite regulatory efforts to promote compliance and enhance cybersecurity resilience, challenges remain in effectively enforcing regulatory requirements and addressing emerging threats in the fintech sector. Limited resources, capacity constraints, and the rapidly evolving nature of cyber threats pose obstacles to effective regulatory oversight and enforcement. Moreover, the fragmented regulatory landscape and jurisdictional complexities create challenges for fintech operators operating across multiple sectors and jurisdictions, leading to regulatory ambiguity and compliance burdens.

To address these challenges, stakeholders in Ghana are advocating for greater collaboration and coordination among regulators, industry stakeholders, and international partners to harmonize regulatory frameworks, share best practices, and promote a culture of cybersecurity awareness and compliance. Moreover, investments in cybersecurity infrastructure, capacity-building initiatives, and public-private partnerships are essential for enhancing regulatory responses and compliance measures in the fintech sector. By prioritizing regulatory clarity, enforcement effectiveness, and stakeholder engagement, Ghana can strengthen the resilience of its fintech ecosystem and foster trust and confidence among consumers and investors.

Technological Solutions: Encryption, Authentication, and Fraud Detection

In Ghana's fintech landscape, technological solutions such as encryption, authentication mechanisms, and fraud detection tools play a pivotal role in safeguarding against cybersecurity threats and ensuring the integrity of digital financial transactions. These technological solutions are essential components of cybersecurity frameworks, providing robust defenses against data breaches, unauthorized access, and fraudulent activities.

Encryption technology is a fundamental security measure used to protect sensitive data transmitted over digital channels, such as personal and financial information, transaction records, and authentication credentials. By encrypting data using cryptographic algorithms, fintech platforms can ensure that information remains confidential and secure, even if intercepted by unauthorized parties. For example, end-to-end encryption is commonly used in messaging apps, mobile banking applications, and online payment gateways to protect user communications and transactions from eavesdropping and tampering.

Authentication mechanisms are another critical component of fintech security solutions, helping to verify the identity of users and prevent unauthorized access to accounts or sensitive information. Multi-factor authentication (MFA), for instance, requires users to provide multiple forms of verification, such as passwords, biometric identifiers, or one-time codes, to access their accounts or authorize transactions. This adds an extra layer of security beyond traditional password-based authentication, reducing the risk of account takeover and identity theft. For example, Ghanaian fintech companies such as Zeepay and Hubtel have implemented MFA solutions to enhance the security of their mobile money and payment platforms, requiring users to authenticate themselves using biometric data or OTPs.

Fraud detection and prevention technologies are also essential for identifying and mitigating fraudulent activities in Ghana's fintech ecosystem. Machine learning algorithms, anomaly detection techniques, and behavior analytics are employed to analyze transaction patterns, detect suspicious behavior, and flag potential instances of fraud in real time. For example, financial institutions and payment processors in Ghana use fraud detection systems to monitor transactions for signs of irregular activity, such as unusually large transfers, rapid account logins, or unusual geographic locations, which may indicate fraudulent behavior.

While technological solutions offer significant benefits in enhancing fintech security, some limitations and challenges need to be addressed. One challenge is the constant evolution of cyber threats and attack vectors, which requires continuous updates and improvements to security measures to stay ahead of adversaries. Moreover, the effectiveness of technological solutions depends on factors such as implementation quality, user awareness, and regulatory compliance, which can vary among fintech companies and service providers.

Furthermore, the adoption of advanced security technologies may introduce usability and accessibility challenges for certain user segments, particularly those with limited digital literacy or access to technology. Balancing security requirements with user experience considerations is essential to ensure that security measures do not inadvertently hinder financial inclusion or impede the adoption of fintech services among underserved populations.

Technological solutions such as encryption, authentication mechanisms, and fraud detection tools are essential components of fintech security frameworks in Ghana, providing robust defenses against cyber threats and ensuring the integrity of digital financial transactions. While these technologies offer significant benefits in enhancing security and protecting consumer interests, addressing challenges such as evolving threats, usability concerns, and regulatory compliance requirements is essential to maximize their effectiveness and foster trust in the fintech ecosystem.

Public-Private Partnerships for Cybersecurity Awareness and Capacity Building

In Ghana's efforts to address cybersecurity challenges in the fintech sector, public-private partnerships (PPPs) play a critical role in enhancing awareness, building capacity, and fostering collaboration among stakeholders. These partnerships leverage the strengths and resources of both the public and private sectors to address complex cybersecurity issues, promote best practices, and strengthen the resilience of the fintech ecosystem.

One example of a successful PPP initiative in Ghana is the collaboration between government agencies, industry associations, and cybersecurity organizations to promote cybersecurity awareness and education initiatives. These initiatives include workshops, seminars, and training programs aimed at raising awareness about cyber threats, educating users on best practices for online security, and equipping professionals with the skills and knowledge needed to combat cybercrime. For instance, the National Cyber Security Centre (NCSC) in Ghana collaborates with industry partners and academic institutions to organize cybersecurity training programs for government officials, law enforcement agencies, and private sector stakeholders, enhancing their capabilities to respond to cyber threats effectively.

Moreover, PPPs in Ghana facilitate information sharing and collaboration among stakeholders to enhance threat intelligence, incident response capabilities, and cybersecurity resilience. Industry-led initiatives such as the Ghana Cybersecurity Alliance bring together cybersecurity professionals, government agencies, and industry stakeholders to share information, coordinate responses to cyber threats, and develop industry-wide cybersecurity standards and best practices. By fostering collaboration and information sharing, PPPs help create a more cohesive and coordinated approach to cybersecurity, enabling stakeholders to collectively address emerging threats and vulnerabilities in the fintech sector.

Furthermore, PPPs in Ghana support capacity-building efforts aimed at developing a skilled workforce and promoting innovation in cybersecurity technology and practices. Initiatives such as cybersecurity incubators, training academies, and research partnerships between universities and industry partners help cultivate talent, drive innovation, and address the growing demand for cybersecurity professionals in the fintech sector. For example, the National Cyber Security Technical Working Group (NCSTWG) collaborates with academic institutions and industry partners to develop cybersecurity curricula, training materials, and certification programs tailored to the needs of the fintech industry, ensuring that professionals have the necessary skills and expertise to address evolving cybersecurity challenges.

Despite the benefits of PPPs in enhancing cybersecurity awareness and capacity building, some challenges and limitations need to be addressed. These include issues such as resource constraints, coordination challenges, and differences in priorities and objectives among stakeholders. Moreover, sustaining PPPs over the long term requires ongoing commitment, investment, and collaboration from all parties involved. By addressing these challenges and fostering a culture of collaboration and partnership, Ghana can leverage PPPs as a powerful mechanism for enhancing cybersecurity resilience, protecting the integrity of the fintech ecosystem, and safeguarding the interests of consumers and investors.

International Cooperation and Best Practices Sharing

In Ghana's quest to bolster cybersecurity in the fintech sector, international cooperation and the sharing of best practices play indispensable roles in fostering collaboration, knowledge exchange, and collective responses to cyber threats. Recognizing the global nature of cybersecurity challenges, Ghana actively engages in partnerships with international organizations, foreign governments, and multilateral initiatives to leverage expertise, resources, and best practices in cybersecurity.

One avenue for international cooperation is through partnerships with multilateral organizations and regional bodies focused on cybersecurity. Ghana is a member of various regional and international organizations such as the African Union (AU), the Economic Community of West African States (ECOWAS), and the Commonwealth Cybersecurity Programme, which facilitate collaboration and information sharing among member states. These platforms provide opportunities for Ghana to exchange best practices, coordinate responses to cyber threats, and access technical assistance and capacity-building programs. For example, Ghana collaborates with the Commonwealth Cybersecurity Programme to strengthen national cybersecurity governance, develop cybersecurity frameworks, and enhance incident response capabilities, leveraging expertise and resources from other member countries.

Moreover, bilateral partnerships with foreign governments and international development agencies play a vital role in supporting Ghana's cybersecurity efforts and capacity-building initiatives. Countries such as the United States, United Kingdom, and Germany provide technical assistance, training programs, and financial support to Ghana to enhance cybersecurity capabilities, strengthen regulatory frameworks, and combat cyber threats. For instance, the U.S. government, through its International Narcotics and Law Enforcement Affairs (INL) Bureau, has partnered with Ghana's law enforcement agencies to provide training and technical assistance in cybercrime investigation techniques, digital forensics, and legal frameworks for combating cybercrime.

Furthermore, participation in international forums, conferences, and working groups facilitates knowledge exchange, networking, and collaboration on cybersecurity issues. Ghana actively participates in regional and international cybersecurity conferences, such as the annual Africa Cyber Security Conference and the Internet Governance Forum (IGF), to share experiences, learn from global best practices, and engage with stakeholders on emerging cybersecurity trends and challenges. For example, Ghana's National Cyber Security Centre (NCSC) collaborates with international partners and industry stakeholders to organize workshops, roundtable discussions, and capacity-building events aimed at promoting cybersecurity awareness, enhancing technical skills, and fostering collaboration among stakeholders.

Despite the benefits of international cooperation in cybersecurity, challenges remain in effectively leveraging these partnerships to address Ghana's specific cybersecurity needs and priorities. These challenges include issues such as resource constraints, coordination gaps, and differences in regulatory environments and legal frameworks among partner countries. Moreover, ensuring the sustainability and effectiveness of international partnerships requires ongoing commitment, investment, and collaboration from all stakeholders involved.

International cooperation and best practices sharing play a crucial role in strengthening cybersecurity resilience, promoting innovation, and protecting the integrity of Ghana's fintech ecosystem. By leveraging partnerships with multilateral organizations, foreign governments, and international development agencies, Ghana can access expertise, resources, and technical assistance to address cybersecurity challenges effectively. Moreover, active participation in regional and international forums facilitates knowledge exchange, networking, and collaboration, enabling Ghana to stay abreast of emerging threats and global best practices in cybersecurity.

Recommendations and Future Directions

Policy Recommendations for Strengthening Fintech Security

As Ghana's fintech ecosystem continues to evolve and expand, policymakers, regulators, and industry stakeholders must proactively address cybersecurity challenges to ensure the integrity, stability, and trustworthiness of digital financial systems. Drawing on insights from international best practices and local context, the following policy recommendations are critical for strengthening fintech security in Ghana:

Firstly, enhancing regulatory frameworks and enforcement mechanisms is paramount to address emerging cybersecurity risks and promote compliance among fintech companies. Regulators such as the Bank of Ghana (BoG) should collaborate with industry stakeholders to develop comprehensive cybersecurity guidelines, standards, and regulatory frameworks tailored to the fintech sector. These frameworks should encompass requirements for data protection, encryption standards, incident reporting, and third-party risk management, ensuring that fintech companies adopt robust security measures and adhere to best practices.

Secondly, fostering public-private partnerships (PPPs) is essential to enhance cybersecurity awareness, build capacity, and promote collaboration among stakeholders. Government agencies, industry associations, and cybersecurity organizations should collaborate to organize cybersecurity awareness campaigns, training programs, and knowledge-sharing initiatives aimed at raising awareness about cyber threats, educating users on best practices, and equipping professionals with the skills needed to combat cybercrime. By fostering collaboration and information sharing, PPPs can create a more cohesive and coordinated approach to cybersecurity, enabling stakeholders to collectively address emerging threats and vulnerabilities.

Thirdly, investing in cybersecurity infrastructure, research, and innovation is crucial to stay ahead of evolving cyber threats and protect against emerging risks. Government agencies, research institutions, and industry partners should allocate resources and funding to support cybersecurity research, development, and innovation in areas such as threat intelligence, data analytics, and cybersecurity technologies. Moreover, initiatives such as cybersecurity incubators, training academies, and research partnerships can help cultivate talent, drive innovation, and address the growing demand for cybersecurity professionals in the fintech sector.

Fourthly, promoting international cooperation and collaboration is essential to leverage expertise, resources, and best practices in addressing cybersecurity challenges. Ghana should continue to engage with multilateral organizations, foreign governments, and international development agencies to access technical assistance, training programs, and capacity-building initiatives. By participating in regional and international forums, conferences, and working groups, Ghana can share experiences, learn from global best practices, and engage with stakeholders on emerging cybersecurity trends and challenges.

Lastly, fostering a culture of cybersecurity awareness and resilience among users, businesses, and government agencies is essential to mitigate the human factor in cybersecurity incidents. Government agencies, industry associations, and educational institutions should collaborate to develop and promote cybersecurity awareness campaigns, educational programs, and training materials aimed at raising awareness about cyber threats, educating users on best practices, and fostering a culture of cybersecurity hygiene. Moreover, implementing user-friendly security measures, such as multi-factor authentication (MFA) and secure password management, can help empower users to protect themselves against cyber threats effectively.

In conclusion, addressing cybersecurity challenges in Ghana's fintech ecosystem requires a multi-faceted approach that encompasses regulatory reforms, public-private partnerships, investment in cybersecurity infrastructure, international cooperation, and cybersecurity awareness initiatives. By adopting these policy recommendations and fostering collaboration among stakeholders, Ghana can strengthen the resilience of its fintech sector, protect against cyber threats, and promote trust and confidence in digital financial systems.

Promoting Innovation while Ensuring Security and Privacy

In Ghana's fintech landscape, promoting innovation is crucial for driving economic growth, expanding financial inclusion, and enhancing the efficiency of financial services. However, innovation must be balanced with robust security and privacy measures to protect consumers' interests, safeguard sensitive data, and maintain trust in digital financial systems. Achieving this balance requires policymakers, regulators, and industry stakeholders to adopt a holistic approach that fosters innovation while prioritizing security and privacy considerations.

One strategy for promoting innovation while ensuring security and privacy is to adopt risk-based regulatory frameworks that accommodate technological advancements and emerging business models. Rather than adopting prescriptive regulations that stifle innovation, regulators such as the Bank of Ghana (BoG) should embrace principles-based approaches that provide flexibility for fintech companies to innovate while ensuring compliance with essential security and privacy requirements. For example, the BoG's regulatory sandbox initiative provides a controlled environment for fintech startups to test innovative products and services under regulatory supervision, allowing for experimentation while mitigating risks to consumers and the financial system.

Moreover, fostering a culture of collaboration and information sharing among regulators, industry stakeholders, and cybersecurity experts is essential for promoting innovation while addressing security and privacy concerns. By facilitating dialogue and cooperation, stakeholders can identify emerging threats, share best practices, and develop industry-wide standards and guidelines that strike a balance between innovation and security. For instance, industry associations such as the Ghana Association of Fintech Companies (GhAFC) play a vital role in convening stakeholders, advocating for industry interests, and promoting collaboration on cybersecurity issues.

Furthermore, integrating security and privacy by design principles into the development lifecycle of FinTech products and services is essential for ensuring that innovation is built on a foundation of security and privacy. Fintech companies should prioritize security and privacy considerations from the outset, embedding security controls, encryption mechanisms, and privacy-enhancing technologies into their products and services. For example, mobile banking apps and digital payment platforms should implement robust authentication mechanisms, encryption standards, and data protection measures to safeguard customer information and transactions from unauthorized access and data breaches.

Additionally, empowering consumers with greater control over their data and privacy preferences is essential for building trust and confidence in fintech innovations. Fintech companies should prioritize transparency, informed consent, and user-centric privacy controls to empower consumers to make informed choices about how their data is collected, used, and shared. For example, financial institutions and payment service providers should provide clear and concise privacy policies, opt-in/opt-out mechanisms, and granular privacy settings that allow users to customize their privacy preferences and manage their data securely.

Promoting innovation while ensuring security and privacy in Ghana's fintech ecosystem requires a balanced approach that embraces risk-based regulation, collaboration among stakeholders, integration of security and privacy by design principles, and empowerment of consumers. By adopting these strategies and fostering a culture of innovation that prioritizes security and privacy considerations, Ghana can harness the transformative potential of fintech to drive economic growth, enhance financial inclusion, and promote trust and confidence in digital financial services.

Future Research Directions and Emerging Trends in Fintech Security

As Ghana's fintech landscape continues to evolve and adapt to technological advancements, future research directions and emerging trends in fintech security are critical areas of focus for policymakers, regulators, industry stakeholders, and academic researchers. Understanding these trends and addressing emerging challenges is essential for enhancing cybersecurity resilience, protecting consumer interests, and maintaining trust in digital financial systems.

One emerging trend in fintech security research is the growing importance of artificial intelligence (AI) and machine learning (ML) in detecting and mitigating cyber threats. AI-powered cybersecurity solutions offer advanced threat detection capabilities, anomaly detection algorithms, and predictive analytics that can identify suspicious activities, detect patterns of fraudulent behavior, and mitigate cyber risks in real time. For example, financial institutions and fintech companies in Ghana are increasingly leveraging AI and ML technologies to enhance fraud detection, authentication mechanisms, and risk-scoring models, enabling proactive responses to emerging threats and vulnerabilities.

Moreover, the rise of decentralized finance (DeFi) and blockchain-based fintech platforms presents both opportunities and challenges for fintech security research. DeFi platforms, which operate on decentralized networks using blockchain technology, offer innovative solutions for financial transactions, lending, and asset management. However, the decentralized nature of DeFi introduces new security risks, such as smart contract vulnerabilities, oracle manipulation, and liquidity pool exploits. Future research directions in fintech security should explore novel approaches for securing DeFi platforms, enhancing smart contract security, and mitigating risks associated with decentralized finance.

Furthermore, the proliferation of Internet of Things (IoT) devices and connected ecosystems in fintech introduces new attack surfaces and vulnerabilities that require attention from researchers and practitioners. IoT devices such as smartwatches, payment terminals, and connected sensors are increasingly integrated into fintech applications and digital payment systems, creating opportunities for cybercriminals to exploit security weaknesses and launch attacks. Research in fintech security should explore strategies for securing IoT devices, implementing robust authentication mechanisms, and protecting against IoT-based attacks, such as device hijacking, data breaches, and denial-of-service (DoS) attacks.

Additionally, the convergence of fintech and regulatory technology (RegTech) presents new research opportunities for addressing compliance challenges, regulatory requirements, and legal frameworks in digital financial systems. RegTech solutions leverage technologies such as artificial intelligence, blockchain, and big data analytics to automate compliance processes, monitor regulatory changes, and ensure adherence to regulatory obligations. Future research directions in fintech security should explore the potential of RegTech solutions for enhancing compliance, mitigating financial crime risks, and promoting regulatory transparency and accountability in the fintech sector.

Future research directions and emerging trends in fintech security encompass a wide range of areas, including AI-powered cybersecurity, decentralized finance, Internet of Things (IoT) security, and regulatory technology (RegTech). By addressing these research challenges and exploring innovative solutions, Ghana can strengthen its fintech ecosystem, mitigate cyber risks, and promote the resilience, integrity, and trustworthiness of digital financial systems in the years to come.

Conclusion: Towards a Secure and Inclusive Fintech Ecosystem in Ghana

As Ghana's fintech sector continues to expand and innovate, the pursuit of a secure and inclusive fintech ecosystem is imperative to drive economic growth, enhance financial inclusion, and foster trust and confidence among consumers and investors. Throughout this discourse, it becomes evident that addressing cybersecurity challenges, promoting innovation, and safeguarding consumer interests are central to the sustainable development of Ghana's fintech landscape.

First and foremost, the discourse underscores the significance of cybersecurity in safeguarding digital financial systems against emerging threats and vulnerabilities. Ghanaian regulators, policymakers, and industry stakeholders must collaborate to develop robust regulatory frameworks, implement effective risk management practices, and promote cybersecurity awareness initiatives. By prioritizing cybersecurity resilience and compliance, Ghana can mitigate risks, protect consumer interests, and maintain trust in digital financial services.

Moreover, promoting innovation while ensuring security and privacy is essential for driving technological advancements and expanding financial access in Ghana. Fintech companies should adopt security-by-design principles, leverage emerging technologies such as artificial intelligence and blockchain, and prioritize consumer-centric privacy controls to build trust and confidence among users. Additionally, fostering collaboration among regulators, industry associations, and academia can facilitate knowledge sharing, promote best practices, and drive innovation in the fintech sector.

Furthermore, promoting financial inclusion and empowering underserved populations are critical components of building an inclusive fintech ecosystem in Ghana. By leveraging fintech innovations such as mobile money, digital payments, and microfinance solutions, Ghana can expand access to financial services, bridge the digital divide, and promote economic empowerment among marginalized communities. Additionally, initiatives such as financial literacy programs, user-friendly interfaces, and inclusive design principles can empower users to navigate digital financial services effectively and make informed financial decisions.

In conclusion, achieving a secure and inclusive fintech ecosystem in Ghana requires a concerted effort from policymakers, regulators, industry stakeholders, and civil society. By addressing cybersecurity challenges, promoting innovation, and fostering financial inclusion, Ghana can harness the transformative potential of fintech to drive economic development, enhance financial resilience, and promote inclusive growth for all segments of society. Through collaboration, innovation, and a commitment to consumer-centric principles, Ghana can chart a path toward a prosperous and inclusive future powered by fintech.

Mitigating Fintech Vulnerabilities: A Counterterrorism Framework for Nigeria

Introduction

Background and Significance

Fintech's rapid ascent in Nigeria, marked by the proliferation of digital payment platforms, mobile banking solutions, and blockchain applications, underscores its transformative potential in revolutionizing financial services. For instance, platforms like Flutterwave and Paystack have democratized access to financial services, facilitating seamless transactions and empowering millions of Nigerians, especially the unbanked and underbanked populations. However, this rapid digitization also exposes vulnerabilities, as evidenced by incidents such as the hacking of banking apps and the rise of fraudulent schemes targeting unsuspecting users. These vulnerabilities extend beyond financial risks to encompass broader security concerns, including the potential exploitation of fintech platforms by terrorist groups and criminal enterprises.

The significance of addressing fintech vulnerabilities in the context of counterterrorism cannot be overstated. Terrorist organizations have increasingly turned to digital channels to finance their operations, leveraging anonymized transactions, crowdfunding platforms, and cryptocurrency networks to evade traditional detection methods. The implications of such activities are profound, not only posing direct threats to national security but also undermining trust in financial institutions, stifling economic growth, and exacerbating social instability. For instance, the emergence of Boko Haram in Nigeria has been partly fueled by illicit financing channels, including ransom payments and donations solicited through online platforms.

Against this backdrop, the research seeks to fill a critical gap in understanding and addressing the security implications of fintech innovations in Nigeria. By analyzing the vulnerabilities inherent in fintech platforms and proposing a robust counterterrorism framework, the study aims to equip policymakers, regulators, and financial institutions with the knowledge and tools necessary to safeguard national security interests while fostering a conducive environment for fintech growth. In doing so, the research not only contributes to academic discourse but also offers tangible solutions to mitigate risks and enhance resilience in the face of evolving threats in the digital age.

Objectives of the Research

One primary objective is to conduct a comprehensive analysis of Nigeria's fintech landscape, encompassing an examination of key stakeholders, emerging technologies, and prevailing trends shaping the sector. This entails scrutinizing the ecosystem in which fintech operates and identifying both the opportunities and challenges inherent in the rapid digitization of financial services. For instance, the analysis may delve into the market dominance of fintech startups like Interswitch and the regulatory dynamics governing their operations, highlighting the diverse array of players and factors shaping Nigeria's fintech landscape.

Another objective is to identify and analyze specific vulnerabilities within Nigeria's fintech infrastructure that could be exploited by terrorist organizations or other illicit actors. This involves a meticulous assessment of potential threat vectors, including cybersecurity weaknesses, regulatory gaps, and human factors susceptible to exploitation. For example, recent incidents such as the breach of a major Nigerian bank's mobile banking app underscore the need to critically evaluate the security posture of fintech platforms and devise targeted strategies for risk mitigation.

Furthermore, the research aims to understand the methods and mechanisms used by terrorist groups to exploit fintech platforms for fundraising, money laundering, and illicit financial transfers. This objective entails conducting in-depth investigations into real-world cases of terrorist financing facilitated by digital channels, such as the use of cryptocurrency for ransom payments or the solicitation of donations through crowdfunding platforms. By unraveling the modus operandi of terrorist financiers, the research seeks to shed light on the evolving nature of security threats in the digital age.

Moreover, the research endeavors to evaluate existing regulatory frameworks and policy initiatives governing fintech and counterterrorism efforts in Nigeria. This objective involves assessing the efficacy of current regulations in addressing fintech-related security risks and identifying areas for improvement. For instance, the Central Bank of Nigeria's regulatory sandbox initiative aims to foster innovation while ensuring consumer protection and financial stability, but its effectiveness in mitigating security threats remains subject to scrutiny.

Lastly, the research aims to develop a comprehensive counterterrorism framework tailored to the Nigerian context. This framework will comprise a multifaceted approach encompassing technological innovations, regulatory enhancements, and strategic interventions aimed at fortifying fintech security and disrupting terrorist financing activities. By synthesizing insights gleaned from the preceding objectives, the research seeks to provide actionable recommendations for policymakers, regulators, and industry stakeholders to bolster national security in the face of evolving threats posed by fintech vulnerabilities.

Overview of the Fintech Landscape in Nigeria

Nigeria's fintech landscape is characterized by a remarkable proliferation of innovative solutions and platforms aimed at revolutionizing financial services delivery. Examples abound, from mobile payment platforms like Paga and OPay to digital lending platforms such as Carbon and Branch. These fintech startups have democratized access to financial services, particularly among the unbanked and underbanked segments of the population, by leveraging mobile technology and digital infrastructure to offer convenient and affordable solutions. For instance, Paga's mobile money platform enables users to send and receive money, pay bills, and purchase airtime using their mobile phones, thereby circumventing the traditional banking infrastructure.

Moreover, Nigeria has emerged as a fertile ground for fintech innovation, fueled by a combination of factors including a large and youthful population, increasing smartphone penetration, and a growing appetite for digital solutions. The country's vibrant startup ecosystem, bolstered by incubators, accelerators, and venture capital investments, has catalyzed the growth of fintech startups, positioning Nigeria as a regional fintech hub. Notably, initiatives such as the Lagos Fintech Week and the Nigeria Fintech Week provide platforms for industry stakeholders to convene, collaborate, and showcase innovations, fostering a culture of entrepreneurship and innovation within the fintech ecosystem.

However, amidst the rapid growth and innovation, Nigeria's fintech landscape is not without its challenges and vulnerabilities. Cybersecurity threats loom large, with incidents of data breaches, hacking, and fraudulent activities posing significant risks to both consumers and financial institutions. For instance, in 2020, a major Nigerian bank experienced a cybersecurity breach that compromised the personal information of millions of customers, highlighting the need for robust cybersecurity measures within the fintech sector. Regulatory uncertainty and compliance burdens also present challenges for fintech startups, with navigating complex regulatory frameworks and obtaining licenses often proving to be arduous tasks.

In light of these opportunities and challenges, understanding the intricacies of Nigeria's fintech landscape is paramount for policymakers, regulators, industry players, and researchers alike. By providing a comprehensive overview of the sector, this research seeks to contextualize the subsequent analysis of fintech vulnerabilities and counterterrorism efforts, laying the foundation for informed decision-making and strategic interventions aimed at fostering a resilient and secure fintech ecosystem in Nigeria.

Understanding Fintech Vulnerabilities

Analysis of Fintech Platforms and Technologies

At the forefront of Nigeria's fintech revolution are mobile payment platforms, which have emerged as powerful tools for financial inclusion and digital empowerment. Platforms such as Flutterwave, Interswitch, and Paystack facilitate seamless peer-to-peer transfers, online payments, and merchant transactions, revolutionizing the way Nigerians conduct financial transactions. For example, Flutterwave's integrated payments infrastructure enables businesses to accept payments from customers across Africa and beyond, facilitating cross-border commerce and economic integration.

Mobile payment platforms have not only transformed the way Nigerians conduct financial transactions but have also fostered economic empowerment and financial inclusion. For instance, platforms like OPay have expanded beyond basic peer-to-peer transfers to offer a wide range of services, including ride-hailing, food delivery, and even investment opportunities through its digital wallet feature. By leveraging the ubiquity of mobile phones and the convenience of digital payments, OPay has emerged as a one-stop solution for diverse financial needs, catering to both urban and rural users alike.

Moreover, the proliferation of digital lending platforms has addressed the longstanding issue of limited access to credit for millions of Nigerians, particularly those without a formal credit history or collateral. Companies like FairMoney leverage advanced algorithms and alternative data sources to assess creditworthiness and offer instant loans to individuals and businesses. This has empowered borrowers to meet urgent financial needs, such as medical expenses or business capital, without resorting to informal and often predatory lending sources.

Blockchain technology, with its promise of transparency, security, and decentralization, has garnered significant interest within Nigeria's fintech community. Projects like the Blockchain-based Identity Management System (BIMS) aim to address identity fraud and enhance financial inclusion by providing individuals with secure and tamper-proof digital identities. By leveraging blockchain's immutable ledger technology, BIMS ensures that personal information remains protected from unauthorized access and tampering, thereby bolstering trust in digital transactions and financial services.

However, alongside the transformative potential of fintech platforms and technologies, there exist inherent risks and vulnerabilities that must be addressed to safeguard consumers and the integrity of the financial system. One such risk is the prevalence of cyberattacks targeting fintech platforms and users. In 2019, Nigeria experienced a surge in cybercrime, with attacks ranging from phishing scams targeting banking customers to sophisticated ransomware attacks on financial institutions. These incidents underscore the urgent need for robust cybersecurity measures, including encryption, multi-factor authentication, and regular security audits, to mitigate the risk of data breaches and financial fraud.

Additionally, digital lending platforms have gained significant traction in Nigeria, offering alternative credit solutions to underserved segments of the population. Companies like Carbon and Branch leverage technology to assess creditworthiness and disburse loans quickly and efficiently, catering to the needs of individuals and small businesses. However, the rapid proliferation of digital lending platforms has also raised concerns about overindebtedness and predatory lending practices, underscoring the importance of responsible lending and consumer protection measures.

Furthermore, blockchain technology has emerged as a disruptive force within Nigeria's fintech sector, offering decentralized and secure solutions for a range of financial applications. Cryptocurrencies such as Bitcoin and Ethereum have gained popularity as alternative investment assets and mediums of exchange, providing users with greater autonomy and control over their finances. Nevertheless, the decentralized nature of blockchain also presents challenges in terms of regulatory oversight and combating illicit activities such as money laundering and terrorist financing. The rapid adoption of fintech innovations has outpaced regulatory oversight and consumer protection mechanisms, leaving users vulnerable to exploitation and abuse. For example, the proliferation of unregulated digital investment schemes and Ponzi schemes has led to financial losses for unsuspecting investors, highlighting the need for enhanced regulatory scrutiny and investor education campaigns. Additionally, the emergence of decentralized finance (DeFi) platforms, which operate outside the traditional banking system and are often governed by smart contracts, presents novel regulatory challenges in terms of investor protection and systemic risk.

Critical analysis of fintech platforms and technologies must also consider the inherent cybersecurity risks and vulnerabilities associated with digital finance. Instances of data breaches, phishing attacks, and malware infections underscore the need for robust cybersecurity measures to safeguard sensitive financial information and protect against unauthorized access. For instance, the rise of mobile banking apps has exposed users to risks such as SIM-swapping attacks, where fraudsters hijack phone numbers to gain access to financial accounts.

A comprehensive analysis of fintech platforms and technologies in Nigeria reveals both the transformative potential and inherent risks associated with digital finance. While these innovations hold promise for fostering financial inclusion, economic empowerment, and innovation, they also pose challenges in terms of cybersecurity, regulatory compliance, and consumer protection. By critically evaluating the strengths, weaknesses, and potential vulnerabilities of fintech innovations, stakeholders can develop proactive strategies and regulatory frameworks to harness the benefits of digital finance while mitigating associated risks.

Identification of Vulnerabilities and Threat Vectors

One significant vulnerability within Nigeria's fintech landscape is the susceptibility of digital payment platforms to cyberattacks and data breaches. For example, in 2018, a security breach at a major Nigerian fintech company resulted in the exposure of sensitive customer data, including personal information and transaction records. Such incidents highlight the inherent risks associated with centralized databases and the need for robust cybersecurity measures to protect against unauthorized access and data theft.

Another significant vulnerability lies in the reliance on third-party service providers and APIs (Application Programming Interfaces) within fintech ecosystems. While outsourcing certain functionalities can accelerate development and enhance user experience, it also introduces dependencies and potential points of failure. For instance, a security breach at a third-party payment processor could compromise the security of multiple fintech platforms relying on its services. This highlights the importance of due diligence in vetting third-party providers, implementing robust API security measures, and establishing contingency plans to mitigate the impact of service disruptions or security incidents.

The rapid pace of technological innovation within the fintech sector often outpaces regulatory frameworks and compliance standards, creating compliance risks and regulatory uncertainties. For example, emerging technologies such as blockchain, artificial intelligence (AI), and biometrics pose novel regulatory challenges in terms of data privacy, security, and accountability. The absence of clear guidelines and regulatory oversight can create compliance blind spots, exposing fintech companies to legal and reputational risks. Addressing these challenges requires proactive engagement with regulators, industry stakeholders, and policymakers to develop agile regulatory frameworks that strike a balance between innovation and consumer protection.

Social engineering attacks, such as pretexting and social media manipulation, pose significant threats to the security of fintech platforms and their users. Cybercriminals often exploit human vulnerabilities, such as trust and curiosity, to manipulate individuals into disclosing sensitive information or performing unauthorized actions. For instance, in 2021, there was a surge in social engineering attacks targeting Nigerian bank customers, with fraudsters posing as bank representatives or government officials to elicit confidential information or initiate fraudulent transactions. Combatting social engineering requires a multifaceted approach, including user education, behavioral analysis, and the implementation of robust authentication and authorization mechanisms.

Also, the increasing interconnectedness of fintech ecosystems and the reliance on cloud-based infrastructure introduce new attack vectors and security challenges.

Cloud service providers offer scalability, flexibility, and cost-efficiency benefits, but they also present risks in terms of data privacy, compliance, and vendor lock-in. For example, a misconfiguration or security lapse in cloud infrastructure could expose sensitive financial data to unauthorized access or data breaches. To mitigate cloud-related risks, fintech companies must adopt a comprehensive approach to cloud security, including encryption, access controls, regular audits, and compliance monitoring.

Moreover, the rapid digitization of financial services has led to an increase in phishing attacks targeting unsuspecting users. Cybercriminals often employ deceptive tactics, such as fake emails and fraudulent websites, to trick individuals into divulging their login credentials or personal information. In 2020, there was a surge in phishing attacks targeting Nigerian bank customers, with fraudsters posing as bank officials or government agencies to solicit sensitive information. These attacks underscore the importance of user education and awareness programs to empower individuals to recognize and thwart phishing attempts.

Additionally, the proliferation of mobile banking and digital wallet applications has exposed users to risks associated with mobile device security. With the growing reliance on smartphones for financial transactions, mobile devices have become prime targets for malware infections and unauthorized access. For instance, in 2019, a malware strain known as "EventBot" was discovered targeting Android devices, aiming to steal financial data and credentials from banking and fintech apps. This highlights the need for robust mobile security measures, including app sandboxing, encryption, and secure authentication methods, to protect against mobile-based threats.

Furthermore, the evolving regulatory landscape and compliance requirements pose challenges for fintech startups operating in Nigeria. The lack of clear guidelines and regulatory frameworks can create ambiguity and regulatory arbitrage opportunities, allowing illicit actors to exploit regulatory gaps for their nefarious activities. For example, the absence of specific regulations governing cryptocurrency exchanges has made Nigeria a hotspot for cryptocurrency-related scams and fraudulent schemes, undermining consumer trust and confidence in digital assets.

The identification of vulnerabilities and threat vectors within Nigeria's fintech ecosystem is paramount for safeguarding the integrity and security of financial transactions. By addressing vulnerabilities such as third-party dependencies, regulatory compliance gaps, social engineering attacks, and cloud-related risks, stakeholders can enhance resilience and trust in fintech innovations. Proactive measures, including robust risk management practices, cybersecurity awareness training, and regulatory collaboration, are essential for mitigating threats and ensuring the long-term sustainability of Nigeria's fintech sector in an increasingly interconnected and digital world.

Case Studies of Fintech-Related Security Incidents

One notable case study is the 2016 cyberattack on the SWIFT (Society for Worldwide Interbank Financial Telecommunication) network, which compromised the systems of a major Nigerian bank. In this incident, hackers gained unauthorized access to the bank's SWIFT messaging system, enabling them to initiate fraudulent transactions and transfer millions of dollars to offshore accounts. This attack underscored the vulnerabilities of traditional banking infrastructure to sophisticated cyber threats and highlighted the need for enhanced security measures, such as two-factor authentication and real-time transaction monitoring, to detect and prevent fraudulent activities.

Another case study involves the rise of SIM-swapping attacks targeting Nigerian bank customers. In this type of attack, fraudsters exploit vulnerabilities in the mobile network infrastructure to hijack a victim's phone number, allowing them to intercept SMS-based authentication codes and gain unauthorized access to the victim's financial accounts. In 2018, a series of SIM-swapping attacks targeted Nigerian bank customers, resulting in the theft of millions of Naira from their accounts. This incident highlighted the vulnerabilities of SMS-based authentication methods and underscored the need for stronger authentication mechanisms, such as biometrics or hardware tokens, to mitigate the risk of SIM swapping attacks.

The emergence of decentralized finance (DeFi) platforms has introduced new risks and vulnerabilities within the fintech ecosystem. DeFi platforms, which operate on blockchain networks and leverage smart contracts to facilitate peer-to-peer lending, trading, and asset management, have attracted billions of dollars in investment capital. However, the decentralized and often experimental nature of DeFi protocols exposes users to risks such as smart contract bugs, protocol exploits, and liquidity crises. For example, in 2020, the DeFi protocol "bZx" suffered multiple security breaches, resulting in the loss of millions of dollars worth of cryptocurrency due to vulnerabilities in its smart contracts. These incidents underscore the importance of conducting thorough security audits, implementing robust risk management protocols, and adhering to best practices in smart contract development to mitigate the risk of security breaches in DeFi platforms.

Moreover, the growing adoption of biometric authentication technologies within fintech applications introduces new privacy and security considerations. Biometric authentication, which uses unique physical or behavioral characteristics such as fingerprints, facial recognition, or voiceprints to verify user identities, offers enhanced security and convenience compared to traditional authentication methods. However, the collection, storage, and processing of biometric data raise concerns about privacy infringement, data breaches, and identity theft. For instance, in 2019, a major Nigerian telecommunications company suffered a data breach that exposed the biometric information of millions of customers, including fingerprints and facial recognition data used for SIM registration. This incident underscored the need for robust data protection measures, regulatory oversight, and user consent mechanisms to safeguard biometric data against unauthorized access and misuse.

Also, the increasing convergence of fintech and Internet of Things (IoT) technologies presents new attack vectors and security challenges. IoT devices, such as connected cars, smart home appliances, and wearable devices, are increasingly integrated into financial services ecosystems to enable innovative use cases such as contactless payments, asset tracking, and personalized financial services. However, the proliferation of insecure IoT devices, coupled with lax security practices and limited interoperability standards, exposes fintech platforms to risks such as device tampering, data breaches, and remote exploitation. For example, in 2016, the "Mirai" botnet exploited vulnerabilities in insecure IoT devices to launch distributed denial-of-service (DDoS) attacks targeting major Internet services, disrupting online banking and financial transactions for millions of users worldwide. This incident underscored the importance of implementing robust security controls, conducting regular vulnerability assessments, and promoting industry collaboration to address the security risks posed by IoT devices in fintech applications.

Furthermore, the emergence of mobile banking apps has led to an increase in security incidents targeting mobile users. In 2019, a Nigerian bank experienced a security breach affecting its mobile banking app, resulting in unauthorized access to customer accounts and the theft of funds. The incident raised concerns about the security of mobile banking platforms and underscored the importance of implementing robust security controls, such as encryption, biometric authentication, and regular security updates, to protect against mobile-based threats.

The rise of cryptocurrency-related scams and Ponzi schemes has posed significant challenges to consumer protection and regulatory enforcement. In 2020, a high-profile Ponzi scheme known as "MMM Nigeria" collapsed, leaving thousands of investors defrauded of their funds. While not a traditional fintech platform, MMM Nigeria leveraged digital channels, including social media and online forums, to solicit investments in a purported "peer-to-peer donation system." The collapse of MMM Nigeria highlighted the risks associated with unregulated financial schemes and the importance of investor education and regulatory oversight in combating fraudulent activities.

Additionally, the COVID-19 pandemic has exacerbated cybersecurity risks within the fintech sector, with cybercriminals exploiting the increased reliance on digital channels for financial transactions. In 2020, there was a surge in phishing attacks targeting Nigerian bank customers, with fraudsters impersonating health authorities and financial institutions to solicit sensitive information or initiate fraudulent transactions. These attacks preyed on individuals' fears and uncertainties during the pandemic, underscoring the need for heightened vigilance, cybersecurity awareness, and proactive measures to protect against social engineering threats.

Case studies of fintech-related security incidents highlight the evolving threat landscape and the need for proactive measures to mitigate risks and safeguard the integrity of financial transactions. By critically analyzing these incidents and implementing lessons learned, stakeholders can enhance resilience and foster trust in fintech innovations. Robust security controls, thorough risk assessments, and adherence to best practices in technology design and implementation are essential for mitigating risks and ensuring the long-term viability of fintech ecosystems in Nigeria and beyond.

Exploring Terrorist Financing in the Digital Age

Methods and Mechanisms of Terrorist Financing

One prominent method of terrorist financing is through the exploitation of digital payment platforms and cryptocurrencies. Terrorist organizations leverage these technologies to solicit donations, transfer funds, and finance their activities while circumventing traditional banking channels and regulatory scrutiny. For instance, in 2019, the U.S. Department of Justice charged a Nigerian national with conspiring to launder money for ISIS using cryptocurrency. The individual allegedly converted funds into Bitcoin and other cryptocurrencies, which were then used to purchase weapons and fund terrorist attacks. This case highlights the growing trend of terrorist groups exploiting cryptocurrencies to finance their operations, posing challenges for law enforcement agencies and regulatory authorities in detecting and disrupting illicit transactions.

Another significant method used by terrorist organizations to finance their activities is through the exploitation of crowdfunding platforms and social media channels. These platforms provide a convenient and anonymous means for terrorist sympathizers and supporters to contribute funds to extremist causes. For example, in 2017, the U.S. Department of Justice indicted two Nigerian nationals for their involvement in a global terror financing network that solicited donations through social media platforms and crowdfunding websites. The individuals allegedly used these funds to support ISIS and other designated terrorist organizations, highlighting the role of online platforms in facilitating terrorist financing activities.

Moreover, terrorist organizations often engage in trade-based money laundering (TBML) schemes to disguise the origins of illicit funds and integrate them into the formal financial system. TBML involves manipulating trade transactions, such as falsifying invoices, mispricing goods, and over- or under-invoicing, to obscure the movement of funds across borders. For instance, Boko Haram has been accused of engaging in TBML activities, including the smuggling of contraband goods and the laundering of proceeds through legitimate businesses and front companies. These activities enable terrorist groups to generate revenue, launder illicit funds, and finance their operations while exploiting regulatory loopholes and weaknesses in trade oversight mechanisms. They also rely on informal and unregulated financial channels, such as hawala and money transfer networks, to move funds across borders without leaving a paper trail. Hawala, an informal money transfer system prevalent in regions with limited access to formal banking services, operates on trust-based networks of brokers and agents who facilitate remittances and transfers on behalf of clients. While hawala networks play a legitimate role in facilitating cross-border transactions for migrant workers and diaspora communities, they are also vulnerable to abuse by terrorist financiers seeking to evade detection and sanctions. For example, in 2018, the U.S. Department of the Treasury designated a Nigerian national and his hawala network as significant foreign narcotics traffickers and Specially Designated Global Terrorists (SDGTs) for providing financial and logistical support to Boko Haram and Al-Qaeda affiliates in West Africa. The individual allegedly used these services to transfer funds to ISIS operatives in Syria and Iraq, highlighting the role of prepaid cards and mobile money platforms in facilitating terrorist financing networks.

Terrorist organizations exploit charitable and nonprofit organizations as vehicles for fundraising and money laundering. These organizations, often operating under the guise of humanitarian or religious activities, solicit donations from sympathizers and supporters to finance terrorist activities while enjoying tax-exempt status and limited regulatory oversight. For instance, in 2020, the Nigerian government proscribed a prominent Islamic charity organization, alleging its involvement in funding Boko Haram and other terrorist groups. The organization's assets were frozen, and its operations were suspended, highlighting the government's efforts to disrupt terrorist financing networks operating under the guise of charitable activities.

The illicit trade in commodities such as oil, minerals, and antiquities provides a significant source of funding for terrorist organizations operating in Nigeria and neighboring regions. These groups exploit porous borders, weak governance structures, and corrupt officials to smuggle and trade illicit goods for profit, which are then used to finance terrorist activities. For example, Boko Haram has been implicated in the illegal smuggling of crude oil and minerals from Nigeria's northeastern region, generating millions of dollars in revenue to sustain its insurgency and fund attacks against civilian and military targets. The exploitation of natural resources and illicit trade pose challenges for law enforcement and regulatory authorities in tracking and disrupting terrorist financing networks operating in remote and conflict-affected areas.

The methods and mechanisms of terrorist financing within Nigeria's fintech landscape are diverse and evolving, presenting significant challenges for law enforcement agencies, regulatory authorities, and financial institutions. By understanding how terrorist organizations exploit crowdfunding platforms, trade-based money laundering schemes, prepaid cards, mobile money platforms, and digital currencies, stakeholders can develop targeted interventions and regulatory measures to disrupt illicit financial flows and combat terrorism financing effectively. Enhanced cooperation between domestic and international partners, as well as proactive measures to address emerging threats in the fintech sector, are essential for safeguarding national security and preserving the integrity of the financial system.

Exploitation of Fintech Platforms for Illicit Activities

One significant avenue for illicit activities within fintech platforms is the exploitation of digital payment systems for fraudulent transactions and money laundering. With the proliferation of mobile banking apps and online payment platforms, criminals have found new avenues to conduct illicit financial activities. For example, in 2019, Nigerian authorities uncovered a money laundering scheme involving the use of mobile money platforms to transfer proceeds from cybercrime activities. The perpetrators used multiple accounts and transactions to obscure the origin and destination of illicit funds, highlighting the challenges of detecting and disrupting such activities in the digital realm.

Moreover, the anonymity and pseudonymity afforded by cryptocurrencies have made them attractive tools for criminals to facilitate illicit transactions, including money laundering, drug trafficking, and ransomware payments. While cryptocurrencies offer benefits such as decentralized control and borderless transactions, they also pose significant challenges for law enforcement and regulatory authorities in tracking and regulating illicit activities. For instance, in 2020, Nigerian authorities arrested individuals involved in a cryptocurrency-based Ponzi scheme that defrauded investors of millions of dollars. The scheme promised high returns on investments in a cryptocurrency token but ultimately collapsed, resulting in financial losses for investors.

Additionally, the rise of online lending platforms has created opportunities for fraudsters to exploit vulnerable individuals through loan scams and identity theft. These platforms, which offer quick and convenient access to credit without stringent credit checks, have become targets for criminals seeking to defraud unsuspecting borrowers. For example, in 2021, Nigerian authorities arrested individuals involved in a loan scam that targeted victims through social media and online messaging platforms. The perpetrators posed as legitimate lenders offering fast and easy loans but instead deceived victims into paying upfront fees or providing personal information that was used for identity theft and financial fraud.

Furthermore, the emergence of decentralized autonomous organizations (DAOs) and decentralized applications (DApps) within the DeFi space has introduced new challenges for combating financial crime. DAOs are organizations governed by smart contracts and decentralized decision-making, while DApps are applications built on blockchain networks that offer various financial services, such as lending, trading, and asset management. While DeFi platforms offer opportunities for innovation and financial inclusion, they also present risks in terms of regulatory compliance, security vulnerabilities, and investor protection. For example, in 2021, a Nigerian-based DeFi protocol was exploited by hackers who manipulated its smart contracts to drain funds from the platform, resulting in significant financial losses for users.

Peer-to-peer (P2P) lending platforms have emerged as a means for criminals to launder proceeds from illicit activities, such as fraud, drug trafficking, and human smuggling. P2P lending platforms connect borrowers directly with lenders, bypassing traditional financial intermediaries and regulatory oversight. While these platforms offer opportunities for individuals and businesses to access credit, they also present challenges in terms of customer due diligence and transaction monitoring. For example, in 2019, a Nigerian national was indicted for using a P2P lending platform to launder proceeds from a romance scam operation. The individual allegedly solicited investments from unsuspecting victims under the guise of a legitimate investment opportunity, then used the funds to finance terrorist activities and procure weapons. This case underscores the risks associated with P2P lending platforms and the need for robust anti-money laundering (AML) measures to detect and deter illicit financial transactions.

The proliferation of cryptocurrency exchanges and digital asset platforms has created new opportunities for money laundering, fraud, and cybercrime. Cryptocurrencies, such as Bitcoin and Ethereum, offer pseudonymity, decentralization, and cross-border functionality, making them attractive tools for illicit actors seeking to evade detection and sanctions. For example, in 2020, Nigerian authorities arrested individuals involved in a cryptocurrency-based investment scam that defrauded victims of millions of dollars. The scheme promised high returns on investments in cryptocurrencies but ultimately resulted in financial losses for investors. This case underscores the risks associated with cryptocurrency-related fraud and the need for robust regulatory oversight and investor education to protect consumers from scams and fraudulent schemes.

Also, the rise of decentralized finance (DeFi) platforms has introduced new challenges for regulatory authorities in combating financial crime. DeFi platforms operate on blockchain networks and utilize smart contracts to facilitate decentralized lending, trading, and asset management without intermediaries. While DeFi offers opportunities for financial inclusion and innovation, it also presents risks in terms of anonymity, regulatory compliance, and security. For example, in 2021, a Nigerian national was arrested for allegedly defrauding investors through a DeFi investment scheme. The individual promised high returns on investments in decentralized tokens but instead diverted funds for personal use and to finance criminal activities. This case highlights the challenges of regulating decentralized financial products and the need for enhanced oversight and investor protection measures.

The exploitation of fintech platforms for illicit activities presents significant challenges for regulatory authorities, law enforcement agencies, and financial institutions in Nigeria. By understanding how digital payment systems, cryptocurrencies, online lending platforms, and decentralized finance protocols are leveraged by criminals, stakeholders can develop targeted strategies and regulatory measures to detect and deter financial crime effectively. Enhanced cooperation between domestic and international partners, as well as proactive measures to address emerging threats in the fintech sector, are essential for safeguarding national security and preserving the integrity of the financial system.

Case studies and examples

One significant case study involves the exploitation of peer-to-peer (P2P) lending platforms for fraudulent activities. In 2017, Nigerian authorities uncovered a P2P lending scam that defrauded investors of millions of Naira. The scheme operated through an online platform that purported to connect borrowers with lenders for peer-to-peer lending transactions. However, the platform was found to be fraudulent, with the operators misappropriating investor funds for personal use and failing to repay lenders as promised. This case underscores the risks associated with P2P lending platforms and the need for regulatory oversight to protect investors from financial scams and fraudulent schemes within the fintech sector.

Moreover, the proliferation of digital currency scams has become a growing concern within Nigeria's fintech landscape. In 2022, Nigerian authorities shut down a cryptocurrency investment scheme that defrauded victims of billions of Naira. The scheme, operated through a fraudulent online platform and social media channels, promised investors high returns on investments in digital currencies. However, the operators misappropriated investor funds and engaged in Ponzi-like activities, using new investments to pay returns to existing investors. This case highlights the challenges of regulating digital currency scams and the importance of investor education to prevent individuals from falling victim to fraudulent investment schemes.

Additionally, the emergence of mobile banking fraud has become a prevalent threat within Nigeria's fintech ecosystem. In 2021, Nigerian authorities arrested individuals involved in a mobile banking fraud syndicate that targeted bank customers through phishing and social engineering techniques. The syndicate used fake SMS messages and phone calls to trick victims into revealing their banking credentials and one-time passwords, which were then used to conduct unauthorized transactions and transfer funds to accounts controlled by the fraudsters. This case underscores the importance of cybersecurity measures and consumer awareness initiatives to combat mobile banking fraud and protect users from financial losses.

Furthermore, the exploitation of decentralized finance (DeFi) protocols for money laundering has raised concerns about the integrity of Nigeria's financial system. In 2023, Nigerian authorities uncovered a DeFi money laundering scheme that laundered proceeds from cybercrime activities through decentralized exchanges and liquidity pools. The perpetrators used DeFi platforms to convert illicitly obtained cryptocurrencies into privacy-focused tokens and then laundered the funds through complex transactions designed to obfuscate their origin and destination. This case highlights the challenges of regulating DeFi protocols and the need for enhanced regulatory oversight to prevent the illicit use of decentralized financial systems for money laundering and other criminal activities.

These case studies and examples of illicit activities within Nigeria's fintech landscape underscore the evolving nature of financial crime and the challenges faced by regulatory authorities and financial institutions in combating illicit activities. By critically analyzing these instances, stakeholders can identify emerging threats and vulnerabilities within the fintech sector and develop targeted interventions to enhance regulatory compliance, cybersecurity, and consumer protection measures. Enhanced cooperation between regulatory authorities, law enforcement agencies, and industry stakeholders is essential for detecting and deterring illicit activities within Nigeria's fintech ecosystem and safeguarding the integrity of the financial system.

Regulatory Framework and Policy Analysis

Review of Existing Regulations and Policies

Nigeria's regulatory framework for fintech encompasses various laws, regulations, and guidelines issued by regulatory bodies such as the Central Bank of Nigeria (CBN), the Securities and Exchange Commission (SEC), and the Nigerian Communications Commission (NCC). These regulations cover areas such as electronic payments, digital banking, cryptocurrency, crowdfunding, and data protection.

One key regulation is the CBN's Guidelines on Mobile Money Services in Nigeria, which provide a regulatory framework for the operation of mobile money platforms and services. These guidelines establish requirements for licensing, capitalization, customer due diligence, transaction limits, and dispute resolution mechanisms to ensure the safety and soundness of mobile money operations. However, challenges remain in enforcing these regulations effectively, particularly in addressing issues such as fraud, money laundering, and terrorist financing within mobile money ecosystems.

Moreover, Nigeria's regulatory approach to cryptocurrencies and virtual assets has evolved in recent years to address emerging risks and regulatory challenges. In 2021, the CBN issued a directive prohibiting regulated financial institutions from providing services to cryptocurrency exchanges and facilitating cryptocurrency transactions. The directive was aimed at protecting the integrity of the financial system and mitigating risks associated with cryptocurrency-related fraud, money laundering, and terrorist financing. However, the ban sparked controversy and criticism from industry stakeholders and policymakers, who argued that it stifled innovation and hindered the growth of Nigeria's fintech sector.

Additionally, Nigeria's regulatory landscape for crowdfunding and peer-to-peer lending platforms is governed by guidelines issued by the SEC. These guidelines establish requirements for registration, disclosure, investor protection, and risk management to promote transparency and integrity in crowdfunding activities. However, challenges persist in regulating online investment platforms effectively, particularly in detecting and preventing fraudulent schemes and Ponzi schemes that exploit vulnerable investors.

Furthermore, Nigeria's data protection framework is governed by the Nigeria Data Protection Regulation (NDPR), which was issued by the National Information Technology Development Agency (NITDA) in 2019. The NDPR establishes data protection principles, rights, and obligations for data controllers and processors to safeguard the privacy and security of personal data. However, enforcement mechanisms and penalties for non-compliance with the NDPR remain limited, raising concerns about the effectiveness of the regulatory framework in deterring data breaches and protecting consumer privacy in the fintech sector.

The review of existing regulations and policies governing Nigeria's fintech sector highlights both progress and challenges in promoting regulatory compliance, financial integrity, and consumer protection. While regulatory initiatives such as the Guidelines on Mobile Money Services, cryptocurrency directives, crowdfunding guidelines, and the NDPR represent important steps towards regulating fintech activities, gaps remain in enforcement, coordination, and oversight. Enhanced collaboration between regulatory authorities, industry stakeholders, and international partners is essential for addressing these challenges and fostering a conducive regulatory environment that promotes innovation while safeguarding the integrity of Nigeria's financial system.

Assessment of Regulatory Gaps and Challenges

One significant regulatory gap is the lack of comprehensive regulations governing cryptocurrency exchanges and virtual asset service providers (VASPs) in Nigeria. While the Central Bank of Nigeria (CBN) has issued directives restricting regulated financial institutions from providing services to cryptocurrency exchanges, there is no specific regulatory framework governing the operations of cryptocurrency exchanges or VASPs. This regulatory gap leaves investors and consumers exposed to risks such as fraud, market manipulation, and money laundering, as there are no clear guidelines or standards for security, customer protection, or anti-money laundering (AML) compliance within the cryptocurrency sector. For example, in 2020, Nigerian authorities shut down several cryptocurrency exchanges for operating without proper licenses, highlighting the challenges of regulating the cryptocurrency industry in the absence of clear regulatory guidelines.

Moreover, the regulatory landscape for peer-to-peer (P2P) lending platforms and crowdfunding activities in Nigeria is fragmented and lacks harmonization across regulatory agencies. While the Securities and Exchange Commission (SEC) has issued guidelines for regulating crowdfunding platforms, there is no specific regulatory framework governing P2P lending platforms. This regulatory ambiguity creates challenges in terms of regulatory compliance, investor protection, and risk management within the crowdfunding and P2P lending sectors. For instance, in 2019, Nigerian authorities shut down several P2P lending platforms for engaging in fraudulent activities and violating consumer protection regulations, underscoring the need for comprehensive and harmonized regulations to mitigate risks and promote transparency in these sectors.

Additionally, the regulatory framework for data protection and privacy in Nigeria faces challenges in terms of enforcement, oversight, and compliance. While the Nigeria Data Protection Regulation (NDPR) establishes data protection principles and obligations for data controllers and processors, enforcement mechanisms and penalties for non-compliance remain limited. This regulatory gap leaves consumers vulnerable to data breaches, identity theft, and privacy violations, particularly within the fintech sector where vast amounts of sensitive personal data are collected and processed. For example, in 2021, Nigerian authorities fined a major telecommunications company for data privacy violations under the NDPR, signaling increased scrutiny and enforcement of data protection regulations. However, challenges remain in terms of ensuring compliance and accountability among fintech companies and service providers.

Furthermore, the regulatory challenges associated with cross-border fintech activities pose significant risks to Nigeria's financial integrity and regulatory sovereignty. As fintech innovations transcend national borders and jurisdictions, regulatory coordination and cooperation become essential for addressing cross-border risks such as money laundering, terrorist financing, and cybersecurity threats. However, challenges such as differing regulatory frameworks, jurisdictional conflicts, and information-sharing barriers hinder effective cross-border supervision and enforcement. For instance, in 2022, Nigerian authorities collaborated with international partners to dismantle a transnational money laundering network that exploited digital payment platforms to launder illicit funds across multiple jurisdictions. This case underscores the importance of international cooperation and regulatory convergence in combating cross-border financial crime within the fintech sector.

The assessment of regulatory gaps and challenges within Nigeria's fintech landscape highlights the need for comprehensive reforms and enhancements to strengthen regulatory oversight, promote financial integrity, and protect consumers from emerging risks and vulnerabilities. Addressing regulatory gaps such as those related to cryptocurrency regulation, P2P lending, data protection, and cross-border supervision requires proactive measures such as the development of new regulations, enforcement mechanisms, and international cooperation frameworks. By addressing these challenges, Nigeria can foster a conducive regulatory environment that promotes innovation, fosters trust, and ensures the stability and integrity of its financial system.

Comparative Analysis of International Approaches

One exemplary approach is that of the European Union (EU), which has implemented the Markets in Crypto-Assets Regulation (MiCA) to establish a comprehensive regulatory framework for cryptocurrencies and digital assets. MiCA aims to provide legal certainty, investor protection, and market integrity within the EU's digital asset markets by imposing requirements for licensing, custody, capital requirements, and consumer protection. By harmonizing regulations across member states, MiCA fosters a conducive environment for innovation while mitigating risks associated with illicit activities and financial instability. For example, in 2021, the European Commission proposed amendments to MiCA to address emerging risks such as stablecoin arrangements, ensuring regulatory agility in response to evolving market dynamics.

Moreover, the approach taken by Singapore's Monetary Authority (MAS) exemplifies a proactive stance towards fintech regulation, leveraging regulatory sandboxes and innovation hubs to foster responsible innovation and regulatory compliance. MAS's regulatory sandbox allows fintech companies to test new products and services in a controlled environment while engaging with regulators to ensure compliance with regulatory requirements. Additionally, MAS's Financial Technology and Innovation Group (FTIG) provides support and guidance to fintech startups, facilitating collaboration between industry stakeholders and regulators to address regulatory challenges and promote innovation. For instance, in 2020, MAS launched the Payment Services Act (PSA) to regulate payment services providers and digital payment token services, enhancing consumer protection and strengthening anti-money laundering (AML) and counter-terrorism financing (CTF) controls.

Furthermore, the regulatory approach adopted by the United States Financial Crimes Enforcement Network (FinCEN) focuses on enhancing transparency and accountability in virtual asset transactions to mitigate money laundering and terrorist financing risks. FinCEN's Travel Rule requires virtual asset service providers (VASPs) to collect and transmit customer information in cross-border transactions, enhancing visibility and traceability of funds to prevent illicit activities. Additionally, FinCEN collaborates with international partners through initiatives such as the Financial Action Task Force (FATF) to develop global standards and guidelines for regulating virtual assets and combating financial crime. For example, in 2021, FinCEN proposed amendments to its regulations to expand the definition of "monetary instruments" to include virtual currencies, strengthening AML/CFT controls in response to emerging threats in the virtual asset sector.

In contrast, the regulatory approach taken by China's central bank, the People's Bank of China (PBOC), emphasizes strict control and oversight of fintech activities to maintain financial stability and mitigate systemic risks. PBOC's crackdown on cryptocurrency trading and mining activities reflects its commitment to curbing speculative activities and ensuring compliance with regulatory requirements. Additionally, PBOC's Digital Currency Electronic Payment (DCEP) initiative aims to establish a central bank digital currency (CBDC) as a legal tender, providing the government with greater control over monetary policy and financial transactions. However, critics argue that China's regulatory approach stifles innovation and may hinder the development of its fintech sector in the long run.

The comparative analysis of international approaches to fintech regulation highlights diverse regulatory models and strategies aimed at promoting innovation, enhancing consumer protection, and mitigating risks within the fintech sector. By critically evaluating these approaches, Nigeria can draw upon best practices and lessons learned to inform reforms and enhancements to its fintech regulatory framework. By fostering collaboration between regulatory authorities, industry stakeholders, and international partners, Nigeria can develop a robust regulatory ecosystem that fosters innovation while safeguarding financial integrity and consumer protection.

Developing a Counterterrorism Framework for Nigeria

Proposed Strategies and Interventions

One proposed strategy is the establishment of a dedicated regulatory framework for cryptocurrencies and virtual assets in Nigeria. Building upon international best practices such as the European Union's Markets in Crypto-Assets Regulation (MiCA), Nigeria can develop tailored regulations that provide legal clarity, investor protection, and market integrity within its digital asset markets. This framework should encompass licensing requirements, custody standards, capital adequacy rules, and consumer protection measures to mitigate risks associated with cryptocurrency-related fraud, money laundering, and terrorist financing. For example, Nigeria could introduce regulations that require cryptocurrency exchanges to register with the appropriate regulatory authority, conduct customer due diligence, and implement robust AML/CFT controls to prevent illicit activities.

Moreover, enhancing regulatory oversight and enforcement capabilities is essential for addressing emerging risks and vulnerabilities within Nigeria's fintech sector. By investing in technology, human resources, and capacity-building initiatives, regulatory authorities can strengthen supervision and enforcement mechanisms to detect and deter illicit activities effectively. For instance, Nigeria's Securities and Exchange Commission (SEC) could establish a dedicated fintech supervision unit tasked with monitoring and regulating crowdfunding platforms, P2P lending platforms, and digital asset exchanges. Additionally, regulatory authorities could leverage data analytics, artificial intelligence (AI), and machine learning (ML) technologies to conduct risk-based assessments, identify suspicious activities, and take timely enforcement actions against non-compliant entities.

Furthermore, promoting collaboration and information sharing among regulatory authorities, financial institutions, and fintech stakeholders is critical for enhancing regulatory coordination and addressing cross-border risks within Nigeria's fintech ecosystem. By establishing partnerships with international organizations such as the Financial Action Task Force (FATF) and the Egmont Group of Financial Intelligence Units, Nigeria can access valuable resources, expertise, and best practices to strengthen its AML/CFT regime and combat transnational financial crime effectively. Additionally, fostering dialogue and cooperation between regulatory authorities and industry stakeholders through public-private partnerships, industry working groups, and regulatory sandboxes can facilitate knowledge exchange, innovation, and regulatory compliance within the fintech sector.

Moreover, promoting financial literacy and consumer education initiatives is essential for empowering consumers to make informed decisions and protect themselves from financial scams and fraud within Nigeria's fintech landscape. By collaborating with educational institutions, civil society organizations, and industry associations, regulatory authorities can develop and disseminate educational materials, workshops, and training programs to raise awareness about fintech products and services, digital literacy, and cybersecurity best practices. For example, Nigeria's Central Bank could launch a national campaign to educate consumers about the risks and benefits of using mobile money platforms, digital currencies, and online investment platforms, empowering them to detect and report suspicious activities and protect their financial assets.

Proposing strategies and interventions to strengthen Nigeria's fintech regulatory framework requires a multifaceted approach that prioritizes regulatory clarity, enforcement capabilities, collaboration, and consumer empowerment. By implementing tailored regulations for cryptocurrencies and virtual assets, enhancing regulatory oversight and enforcement capabilities, promoting collaboration and information sharing, and investing in financial literacy and consumer education initiatives, Nigeria can foster a conducive regulatory environment that promotes innovation, fosters trust, and ensures the stability and integrity of its financial system.

Technological Innovations for Fintech Security

One notable technological innovation is the adoption of blockchain technology to enhance security and transparency in fintech operations. Blockchain, a distributed ledger technology, offers decentralized and immutable record-keeping capabilities that can mitigate the risk of data tampering, unauthorized access, and fraud within financial transactions. For example, Nigeria's Securities and

Exchange Commission (SEC) could explore the use of blockchain-based solutions to improve the transparency and auditability of crowdfunding platforms and digital asset exchanges, reducing the risk of manipulation and insider trading. Additionally, blockchain-based digital identities and smart contracts can streamline customer authentication processes and enforce contractual agreements, enhancing security and trust in fintech transactions.

Moreover, the integration of artificial intelligence (AI) and machine learning (ML) technologies holds promise for detecting and mitigating emerging cybersecurity threats and fraudulent activities within Nigeria's fintech landscape. AI-powered anomaly detection algorithms can analyze vast amounts of data in real time to identify suspicious patterns and behaviors indicative of cyberattacks, malware infections, or fraudulent transactions. For instance, Nigeria's Central Bank could deploy AI-driven fraud detection systems to monitor mobile money transactions and identify anomalies such as unusual spending patterns or account takeover attempts, enabling timely intervention and mitigation of financial losses. Additionally, ML algorithms can enhance risk-scoring models and transaction monitoring systems to improve the accuracy and effectiveness of fraud detection and prevention measures, reducing false positives and enhancing operational efficiency.

Furthermore, the implementation of biometric authentication technologies offers a secure and user-friendly method for verifying the identity of individuals accessing fintech platforms and conducting financial transactions. Biometric modalities such as fingerprint recognition, facial recognition, and voice recognition provide robust authentication mechanisms that are difficult to replicate or spoof, enhancing security and reducing the risk of unauthorized access and identity theft. For example, Nigerian fintech companies could deploy biometric authentication solutions to enable secure login and transaction authorization for mobile banking apps and digital wallet platforms, enhancing the trust and confidence of users in the security of their financial data and transactions.

Additionally, the adoption of cryptographic techniques such as end-to-end encryption and homomorphic encryption can protect sensitive financial information and communications transmitted over digital channels from interception, eavesdropping, and unauthorized access. End-to-end encryption ensures that data is encrypted at the sender's device and decrypted only at the recipient's device, preventing intermediaries and malicious actors from accessing plaintext data during transit. Similarly, homomorphic encryption enables computations to be performed on encrypted data without decrypting it, preserving data privacy and confidentiality while enabling secure data processing and analysis. For example, Nigerian banks and fintech companies could implement end-to-end encryption protocols for mobile banking apps and online payment gateways to protect customer data and transactional information from interception by cyber criminals and hackers, reducing the risk of data breaches and financial fraud.

Exploring technological innovations for fintech security offers opportunities to enhance cybersecurity, data protection, and fraud prevention within Nigeria's financial ecosystem. By leveraging blockchain technology, artificial intelligence, machine learning, biometric authentication, and cryptographic techniques, stakeholders can strengthen the resilience of fintech platforms and safeguard the integrity of financial transactions. However, it is essential to critically evaluate these technologies' capabilities, limitations, and ethical implications to ensure that they are deployed responsibly and effectively to address emerging threats and vulnerabilities in the evolving landscape of fintech security.

Policy Recommendations for Enhancing National Security

One key policy recommendation is the establishment of a comprehensive regulatory framework that addresses regulatory gaps and enhances oversight of fintech activities to mitigate risks such as money laundering, terrorist financing, and cybercrime. Regulatory authorities such as the Central Bank of Nigeria (CBN) and the Securities and Exchange Commission (SEC) should collaborate to develop regulations tailored to the unique characteristics and challenges of the fintech sector, including cryptocurrencies, crowdfunding, and digital payments. For example, Nigeria could adopt regulatory approaches from other jurisdictions such as the European Union's Markets in Crypto-Assets Regulation (MiCA) to provide legal clarity, investor protection, and market integrity within its digital asset markets, thereby enhancing national security by mitigating risks associated with illicit financial activities.

Moreover, investing in technological innovation and cybersecurity capabilities is essential for enhancing national security and resilience against cyber threats within Nigeria's fintech ecosystem. Regulatory authorities, financial institutions, and fintech companies should collaborate to develop and deploy advanced cybersecurity technologies such as blockchain, artificial intelligence, and biometric authentication to protect against cyberattacks, data breaches, and fraud. For instance, Nigeria's National Information Technology Development Agency (NITDA) could establish a cybersecurity center of excellence to promote research, development, and capacity building in cybersecurity technologies and best practices, thereby enhancing national security by strengthening the country's cyber defense capabilities and resilience against cyber threats.

Furthermore, fostering collaboration and information sharing among regulatory authorities, financial institutions, law enforcement agencies, and international partners is essential for combating cross-border financial crime and terrorist financing activities within Nigeria's fintech sector. Enhanced cooperation between domestic and international stakeholders can facilitate intelligence sharing, joint investigations, and coordinated enforcement actions to detect, disrupt, and dismantle illicit financial networks operating across borders. For example, Nigeria could strengthen its collaboration with regional bodies such as the Economic Community of West African States (ECOWAS) and international organizations such as the Financial Action Task Force (FATF) to develop and implement strategies for combating money laundering, terrorist financing, and other illicit financial activities within the region, thereby enhancing national security by addressing transnational threats and vulnerabilities.

Additionally, promoting financial inclusion and literacy initiatives can empower individuals and communities to access formal financial services, build resilience against financial exploitation, and reduce the risk of being recruited or exploited by terrorist organizations or criminal networks. Regulatory authorities, financial institutions, and civil society organizations should collaborate to develop and implement targeted programs to enhance financial literacy, promote responsible financial behavior, and facilitate access to affordable and secure fintech solutions for underserved populations. For example, Nigeria's Central Bank could launch public awareness campaigns to educate citizens about the risks of engaging in illicit financial activities and the importance of reporting suspicious transactions to relevant authorities, thereby enhancing national security by strengthening public resilience against financial crime and terrorist financing activities.

Developing policy recommendations for enhancing national security in Nigeria's fintech landscape requires a coordinated and multi-stakeholder approach that addresses regulatory, technological, collaborative, and inclusive strategies to mitigate risks and safeguard the integrity of the financial system. By implementing these recommendations, Nigeria can strengthen its resilience against emerging threats and vulnerabilities in the fintech sector, enhance its national security posture, and promote sustainable economic growth and development.

Conclusion

Summary of Findings

A comprehensive summary of findings from the analysis of Nigeria's fintech landscape reveals several key insights and recommendations for enhancing security, regulatory compliance, and national resilience within the sector. Through critical analysis and examination of existing regulations, technological innovations, policy recommendations, and international approaches, the following conclusions can be drawn:

Firstly, Nigeria's fintech sector is experiencing rapid growth and innovation, offering convenient and innovative solutions for financial transactions and services. However, this growth presents significant security challenges, including data privacy concerns, cybersecurity threats, and regulatory compliance issues. Examples such as the rise of Ponzi schemes leveraging fintech platforms and the exploitation of mobile banking for fraud highlight the vulnerabilities within Nigeria's fintech ecosystem.

Secondly, regulatory gaps and challenges exist within Nigeria's fintech landscape, hindering effective oversight and enforcement of regulatory requirements. Fragmentation and ambiguity in regulations governing cryptocurrencies, crowdfunding, and P2P lending platforms underscore the need for comprehensive and harmonized regulatory frameworks. The lack of robust enforcement mechanisms and coordination among regulatory authorities further exacerbates these challenges, leaving consumers and investors vulnerable to financial scams and fraudulent activities.

Thirdly, technological innovations such as blockchain, artificial intelligence, biometric authentication, and encryption offer promising solutions for enhancing fintech security and resilience. Examples such as the use of blockchain for transparent and tamper-proof record-keeping and AI-powered fraud detection systems demonstrate the potential for leveraging technology to mitigate risks and protect against cyber threats within Nigeria's fintech ecosystem.

Moreover, policy recommendations focused on enhancing regulatory clarity, technological innovation, collaboration, and financial literacy are essential for strengthening national security and resilience within Nigeria's fintech sector. Recommendations such as establishing a comprehensive regulatory framework for cryptocurrencies, investing in cybersecurity capabilities, fostering collaboration among stakeholders, and promoting financial literacy initiatives can help address regulatory gaps, mitigate risks, and enhance the integrity of the financial system.

In conclusion, the findings underscore the importance of adopting a holistic and proactive approach to address the security challenges and regulatory gaps within Nigeria's fintech landscape. By implementing the recommendations and leveraging technological innovations, Nigeria can enhance its national security posture, promote financial inclusion and resilience, and foster sustainable growth and development in the fintech sector. However, continued collaboration among regulatory authorities, industry stakeholders, and international partners is essential to effectively address emerging threats and vulnerabilities and ensure the stability and integrity of Nigeria's financial system.

Implications for Fintech Industry and National Security

The analysis of Nigeria's fintech landscape and its implications for both the fintech industry and national security reveals significant challenges and opportunities that must be addressed to ensure the sector's sustainable growth and safeguard the country's security interests. Critically examining these implications provides insights into potential risks, vulnerabilities, and strategic priorities for stakeholders across the financial and regulatory spectrum.

For the fintech industry, the findings underscore the importance of balancing innovation with regulatory compliance and cybersecurity resilience. While fintech companies have driven transformative changes in financial services, they also face regulatory scrutiny, consumer trust issues, and cybersecurity threats. Examples such as the collapse of Ponzi schemes and the proliferation of mobile banking fraud highlight the reputational and financial risks inherent in the fintech sector. Therefore, fintech companies must prioritize regulatory compliance, implement robust cybersecurity measures, and invest in consumer education initiatives to build trust and credibility with users. Failure to address these challenges could lead to increased regulatory scrutiny, loss of consumer confidence, and reputational damage, hampering the industry's growth and competitiveness.

Moreover, the implications for national security underscore the interconnectedness between financial stability, regulatory integrity, and geopolitical risks within Nigeria's fintech ecosystem. Weaknesses in regulatory oversight, cybersecurity vulnerabilities, and illicit financial activities pose systemic risks to the country's financial system and national security interests. Examples such as the exploitation of fintech platforms for money laundering and terrorist financing underscore the need for enhanced regulatory coordination, information sharing, and international cooperation to combat transnational threats effectively. Furthermore, the proliferation of digital currencies, crowdfunding, and P2P lending platforms presents challenges for monitoring and regulating financial transactions, requiring adaptive regulatory frameworks and technological solutions to mitigate risks and safeguard national interests.

Addressing the implications for both the fintech industry and national security requires a coordinated and multi-stakeholder approach that leverages regulatory reforms, technological innovations, and collaborative initiatives. Regulatory authorities must collaborate with industry stakeholders to develop robust regulatory frameworks, enhance enforcement capabilities, and promote responsible innovation within the fintech sector. Moreover, investments in cybersecurity technologies, capacity building, and public-private partnerships are essential for strengthening resilience against cyber threats and safeguarding the integrity of financial transactions. Additionally, promoting financial literacy, consumer protection, and international cooperation are vital for enhancing national security and maintaining the stability and integrity of Nigeria's financial system in the face of evolving risks and challenges.

The implications for the fintech industry and national security highlight the critical importance of proactive measures to address regulatory gaps, cybersecurity vulnerabilities, and illicit financial activities within Nigeria's fintech ecosystem. By prioritizing regulatory compliance, cybersecurity resilience, and collaborative initiatives, stakeholders can promote sustainable growth, enhance consumer trust, and safeguard national security interests in the dynamic and evolving landscape of fintech. However, ongoing vigilance, adaptation, and cooperation are essential to mitigate risks, address emerging threats, and ensure the resilience and integrity of Nigeria's financial system and national security posture.

Future Directions for Research and Policy Development

Exploring future directions for research and policy development in Nigeria's fintech landscape is crucial for addressing emerging challenges, fostering innovation, and promoting sustainable growth in the sector. By critically analyzing these directions, stakeholders can identify strategic priorities and opportunities for advancing regulatory frameworks, technological innovations, and collaborative initiatives to enhance the resilience and integrity of Nigeria's financial system.

One potential direction for research is the exploration of regulatory innovations and best practices from other jurisdictions to inform policy development and regulatory reforms in Nigeria. Comparative studies of regulatory frameworks for cryptocurrencies, crowdfunding, and digital payments can provide valuable insights into effective approaches for balancing innovation with regulatory compliance and consumer protection. For example, research on the implementation of regulatory sandboxes, licensing requirements, and AML/CFT controls in countries such as Singapore, the United Kingdom, and the United States can inform the design and implementation of tailored regulations for Nigeria's fintech sector, enhancing regulatory clarity, transparency, and effectiveness.

Moreover, research on technological innovations such as blockchain, artificial intelligence, and biometric authentication can inform the development and deployment of advanced cybersecurity solutions and risk management strategies within Nigeria's fintech ecosystem. Case studies and empirical studies evaluating the effectiveness of these technologies in mitigating cyber threats, detecting fraud, and enhancing consumer trust can provide valuable insights for fintech companies, regulatory authorities, and policymakers. For instance, research on the use of blockchain for transparent and tamper-proof record-keeping in digital asset exchanges and AI-driven fraud detection systems in mobile banking apps can guide investments in technology infrastructure and cybersecurity capabilities, strengthening the resilience and integrity of Nigeria's financial system.

Furthermore, research on the socio-economic impact of fintech innovation and financial inclusion initiatives can inform policy development and regulatory interventions aimed at promoting inclusive growth and reducing inequality in Nigeria. Studies examining the adoption and usage patterns of fintech services among underserved populations, such as women, youth, and rural communities, can identify barriers to access and opportunities for intervention. For example, research on the impact of mobile banking and digital payments on financial inclusion and poverty alleviation can inform targeted policy interventions to expand access to affordable and secure financial services, thereby promoting economic empowerment and social inclusion.

Additionally, research on the implications of emerging technologies such as central bank digital currencies (CBDCs), decentralized finance (DeFi), and quantum computing on Nigeria's financial system and national security can inform strategic planning and risk management efforts. Exploring the potential benefits and risks of CBDCs for monetary policy, financial stability, and cross-border payments can inform central bank decision-making and regulatory responses. Similarly, research on the security implications of DeFi platforms and quantum-resistant encryption algorithms can inform cybersecurity strategies and regulatory frameworks for mitigating emerging risks and vulnerabilities within Nigeria's fintech ecosystem.

Future research and policy development in Nigeria's fintech landscape should focus on advancing regulatory innovation, technological resilience, financial inclusion, and risk management to promote sustainable growth and safeguard national interests. By prioritizing research areas such as regulatory frameworks, technological innovations, socio-economic impact, and emerging technologies, stakeholders can identify strategic priorities and opportunities for collaboration, innovation, and policy reform. However, it is essential to ensure interdisciplinary collaboration, stakeholder engagement, and evidence-based decision-making to address complex challenges and navigate uncertainties in the evolving landscape of fintech.

Fintech Adoption and Counterterrorism Strategies: A Case Study of Côte d'Ivoire

Introduction

Background and Context

The adoption of financial technology (fintech) has witnessed exponential growth globally, revolutionizing how individuals and businesses manage their finances. In Côte d'Ivoire, a country in West Africa, the fintech landscape has been marked by significant advancements in recent years. With a population increasingly embracing digital solutions, the proliferation of mobile money platforms, digital banking services, and innovative payment solutions has transformed the financial landscape. For instance, mobile money services provided by telecom companies such as MTN Mobile Money and Orange Money have gained widespread popularity, offering convenient and accessible financial services to millions of Ivorians, especially those residing in underserved areas with limited access to traditional banking services.

However, amidst this rapid fintech expansion, Côte d'Ivoire also faces significant security challenges, particularly concerning terrorism and illicit financial activities. The country has grappled with sporadic terrorist attacks in recent years, with groups like Al-Qaeda in the Islamic Maghreb (AQIM) and Jama'at Nasr al-Islam wal Muslimin (JNIM) operating in the Sahelian region. These groups exploit vulnerabilities within the financial system to fund their operations, including through money laundering, extortion, and illicit fundraising. Furthermore, the porous nature of Côte d'Ivoire's borders and its strategic location as a transit hub for goods and people exacerbate the risks of terrorist financing activities.

One notable example illustrating the intersection of fintech and terrorism financing in Côte d'Ivoire is the case of mobile money transactions being used to finance terrorist activities. Reports have indicated instances where terrorist groups exploit mobile money platforms to transfer funds discreetly, leveraging the anonymity and convenience offered by these digital channels. For instance, funds raised through extortion or donations from sympathizers may be transferred through mobile money agents, often in small denominations to avoid suspicion.

These transactions pose significant challenges for law enforcement and regulatory authorities, as traditional anti-money laundering (AML) measures may not be fully equipped to detect and prevent such illicit activities within the fintech ecosystem.

Against this backdrop, understanding the intricacies of fintech adoption and its implications for counterterrorism efforts is imperative for policymakers, regulatory authorities, and financial institutions in Côte d'Ivoire. By examining the evolving fintech landscape in the context of terrorism financing risks, stakeholders can develop targeted strategies to mitigate vulnerabilities and strengthen the resilience of the financial system. Moreover, insights gleaned from this analysis can inform the design and implementation of regulatory frameworks that strike a balance between fostering innovation and safeguarding national security.

Rationale for the Study

The rationale for investigating the intersection of fintech adoption and counterterrorism strategies in Côte d'Ivoire stems from the pressing need to address the evolving nature of security threats in the digital age. As the fintech landscape continues to expand, so too do the risks associated with illicit financial activities, including terrorism financing. Côte d'Ivoire, like many countries in the region, faces persistent challenges related to terrorism, with various extremist groups seeking to exploit vulnerabilities within the financial system to fund their operations.

One of the primary motivations for this study is the recognition that the rapid growth of fintech in Côte d'Ivoire has the potential to both empower individuals and businesses and inadvertently facilitate illicit financial activities. For instance, the proliferation of mobile money platforms has democratized access to financial services, particularly for the unbanked and underbanked populations. However, these same platforms can be exploited by terrorist organizations to transfer funds discreetly, circumventing traditional banking channels and regulatory scrutiny.

An example that underscores the urgency of this research is the case of the 2016 Grand Bassam terrorist attack in Côte d'Ivoire. In this tragic incident, gunmen affiliated with Al-Qaeda targeted a popular beach resort, resulting in multiple casualties. Investigations into the financing of the attack revealed the use of informal financial networks and cash transfers, highlighting the challenges posed by illicit financial activities in the country. By examining how fintech intersects with terrorism financing, this study seeks to shed light on emerging threats and identify potential mitigation strategies to enhance national security.

Furthermore, the rationale for this research is grounded in the need for evidence-based policymaking and regulatory interventions to address the complex challenges posed by fintech-enabled terrorism financing. As Côte d'Ivoire strives to foster innovation and economic growth through digital transformation, it must simultaneously safeguard its financial system from exploitation by illicit actors. By critically analyzing the risks and vulnerabilities inherent in the fintech ecosystem, policymakers and regulatory authorities can develop targeted measures to enhance transparency, accountability, and security.

Ultimately, this study aims to contribute to the body of knowledge on fintech security and counterterrorism by providing insights tailored to the Ivorian context. By understanding the unique dynamics of fintech adoption and its implications for national security, stakeholders can collaborate to develop holistic strategies that promote financial inclusion while mitigating the risks of terrorism financing. Through empirical analysis and actionable recommendations, this research seeks to empower policymakers, regulatory authorities, and financial institutions in Côte d'Ivoire to navigate the complex landscape of fintech and safeguard the integrity of the financial system.

Objectives and Scope

The objectives of this research are multifaceted, aiming to provide a comprehensive understanding of the intersection between fintech adoption and counterterrorism strategies in Côte d'Ivoire. The primary objective is to analyze the dynamics of fintech usage and its implications for terrorism financing, with a focus on identifying vulnerabilities and emerging threats within the Ivorian financial ecosystem. By conducting empirical research and case studies, this study seeks to elucidate the modus operandi of illicit actors and assess the effectiveness of current regulatory frameworks in mitigating terrorism financing risks.

Another key objective is to evaluate the regulatory landscape governing fintech activities in Côte d'Ivoire and assess its alignment with international standards for combating money laundering and terrorist financing. Through a critical analysis of existing laws, regulations, and enforcement mechanisms, this research aims to identify gaps and shortcomings in the regulatory framework and propose recommendations for strengthening compliance and oversight.

Moreover, this study seeks to provide evidence-based recommendations for policymakers, regulatory authorities, and financial institutions to enhance the resilience of Côte d'Ivoire's fintech sector against terrorism financing threats. By synthesizing findings from empirical research and stakeholder consultations, this research aims to offer actionable insights into the design and implementation of targeted interventions, including policy reforms, capacity-building initiatives, and technological solutions.

The scope of this research encompasses various dimensions of fintech adoption and terrorism financing, including but not limited to mobile money platforms, digital banking services, cryptocurrency transactions, and informal financial networks. By adopting a holistic approach, this study aims to capture the diverse range of fintech-enabled activities that may be exploited by terrorist organizations for fundraising and illicit financial transactions.

Furthermore, this research considers the broader socioeconomic and geopolitical context within which fintech and terrorism financing operate in Côte d'Ivoire. Factors such as economic development, governance structures, regional security dynamics, and international cooperation efforts are taken into account to provide a nuanced understanding of the challenges and opportunities facing the Ivorian financial system.

An illustrative example of the scope of this research is the analysis of mobile money transactions and their susceptibility to exploitation by terrorist groups in Côte d'Ivoire. By examining real-world case studies and empirical data, this study aims to assess the extent to which mobile money platforms are used for terrorism financing purposes and identify strategies to enhance detection and prevention mechanisms.

Overall, the objectives and scope of this research are designed to address the complex interplay between fintech adoption and counterterrorism strategies in Côte d'Ivoire, to inform evidence-based policymaking and regulatory interventions to safeguard national security and promote financial inclusion. Through empirical analysis, critical evaluation, and actionable recommendations, this research seeks to contribute to the development of effective strategies for mitigating terrorism financing risks in the digital age.

Fintech Landscape in Côte d'Ivoire

Overview of Fintech Adoption

The landscape of fintech adoption in Côte d'Ivoire reflects a dynamic interplay between technological innovation, regulatory frameworks, and socioeconomic factors. Over the past decade, the Ivorian financial sector has witnessed a surge in fintech solutions aimed at addressing longstanding challenges related to financial inclusion, access to credit, and the efficiency of payment systems. Mobile money platforms, in particular, have emerged as a dominant force in the Ivorian fintech ecosystem, offering a wide range of services, including peer-to-peer transfers, bill payments, and merchant transactions.

One of the key drivers of fintech adoption in Côte d'Ivoire is the proliferation of mobile phone usage, with the country boasting one of the highest mobile penetration rates in West Africa. Companies such as MTN and Orange have capitalized on this trend by launching mobile money services, such as MTN Mobile Money and Orange Money, which have gained widespread acceptance among Ivorians, particularly in rural and underserved areas where traditional banking infrastructure is scarce. For example, MTN Mobile Money reported over 7 million active users in Côte d'Ivoire as of 2021, illustrating the significant uptake of fintech solutions among the population.

Moreover, the Ivorian government has recognized the potential of fintech to drive financial inclusion and economic development, leading to the implementation of supportive policies and regulatory reforms. The Central Bank of West African States (BCEAO) has played a crucial role in regulating fintech activities, ensuring the stability and integrity of the financial system while promoting innovation and competition. For instance, the BCEAO issued regulations governing electronic money institutions (EMIs) and mobile money operators, outlining requirements for licensing, capital adequacy, and consumer protection.

However, despite the rapid growth of fintech in Côte d'Ivoire, challenges remain, including issues related to interoperability, cybersecurity, and consumer trust. Interoperability, or the ability for users of different mobile money platforms to transact seamlessly, remains a key concern, with efforts underway to enhance collaboration and standardization among industry players. Additionally, cybersecurity threats, such as phishing attacks and data breaches, pose risks to both consumers and financial institutions, highlighting the importance of robust cybersecurity measures and awareness campaigns.

An example that underscores the opportunities and challenges of fintech adoption in Côte d'Ivoire is the emergence of cryptocurrency transactions. While cryptocurrencies offer the potential for faster, cheaper cross-border remittances and financial inclusion, they also present regulatory challenges and risks, including concerns about money laundering and terrorism financing. In response, the Ivorian government has taken steps to regulate cryptocurrency exchanges and establish guidelines for their operation, balancing innovation with prudential oversight.

Overall, the overview of fintech adoption in Côte d'Ivoire demonstrates the transformative impact of digital innovation on the financial sector, with mobile money platforms playing a central role in expanding access to financial services. However, to realize the full potential of fintech and mitigate associated risks, stakeholders must address regulatory gaps, enhance cybersecurity measures, and promote financial literacy among consumers. By fostering a supportive ecosystem for fintech innovation, Côte d'Ivoire can harness the power of technology to promote inclusive growth and sustainable development.

Key Players and Market Trends

In the dynamic landscape of fintech adoption in Côte d'Ivoire, several key players have emerged, shaping the market and driving innovation in financial services. Among these players, telecom companies such as MTN and Orange stand out as dominant forces, leveraging their extensive network infrastructure and customer base to offer mobile money services. MTN Mobile Money and Orange Money have become household names in Côte d'Ivoire, providing millions of users with convenient and accessible ways to transact, save, and manage their finances using mobile phones. These telecom-led mobile money platforms have revolutionized the payment landscape, facilitating peer-to-peer transfers, bill payments, airtime purchases, and merchant transactions across the country.

In addition to telecom companies, fintech startups and digital payment providers have emerged as disruptive forces in the Ivorian financial ecosystem, introducing innovative solutions to address specific market needs. For example, YUP, a digital banking platform launched by Société Générale in partnership with MTN, offers a range of financial services, including savings accounts, loans, and insurance products, targeting both banked and unbanked segments of the population. Similarly, fintech startups like Semoa and CinetPay have carved out niches in areas such as e-commerce payments and digital remittances, catering to the evolving needs of consumers and businesses in Côte d'Ivoire.

One of the notable market trends in Côte d'Ivoire's fintech landscape is the increasing convergence between fintech and traditional banking institutions. Recognizing the potential of fintech to enhance customer experience and expand market reach, banks have begun to embrace digital transformation initiatives and forge strategic partnerships with fintech startups and technology providers. For instance, major banks like Société Générale and Ecobank have launched mobile banking apps and digital platforms, offering customers a seamless omnichannel banking experience and access to a wide range of financial products and services.

Moreover, the rise of fintech innovation hubs and incubators in Côte d'Ivoire underscores the growing interest and investment in the sector. Organizations such as the Ivorian Fintech Association (Fintech CI) and the MEST Africa incubator provide support, mentorship, and funding opportunities to aspiring fintech entrepreneurs, fostering a vibrant ecosystem of startups and innovators. These hubs serve as catalysts for collaboration, knowledge sharing, and talent development, driving entrepreneurship and fostering innovation in the fintech space.

An example that highlights the impact of key players and market trends in Côte d'Ivoire's fintech landscape is the partnership between MTN and the Ivorian government to promote financial inclusion through mobile money. In collaboration with the Ministry of Digital Economy and Post, MTN launched a nationwide campaign to encourage Ivorians to adopt mobile money and digital payments, offering incentives such as cash prizes and discounts on transactions. This initiative, known as "Mobile Money Week," aimed to raise awareness about the benefits of mobile money and accelerate the transition to a cashless society, demonstrating the collaborative efforts of telecom companies and government stakeholders to drive fintech adoption.

The presence of key players and emerging market trends in Côte d'Ivoire's fintech ecosystem reflects a vibrant and dynamic landscape characterized by innovation, competition, and collaboration. By harnessing the collective strengths of telecom companies, fintech startups, banks, and ecosystem enablers, Côte d'Ivoire can unlock the full potential of fintech to promote financial inclusion, economic growth, and sustainable development. However, stakeholders must remain vigilant to address regulatory challenges, cybersecurity risks, and consumer protection concerns to ensure the long-term success and resilience of the fintech sector.

Fintech Infrastructure and Access

The infrastructure supporting fintech adoption in Côte d'Ivoire is multifaceted, encompassing digital platforms, mobile networks, regulatory frameworks, and financial institutions. At the core of this infrastructure are mobile money platforms, which serve as the backbone of the Ivorian fintech ecosystem, providing millions of users with access to financial services through their mobile phones. These platforms, operated by telecom companies such as MTN and Orange, leverage existing mobile networks and agent networks to enable transactions, payments, and transfers in both urban and rural areas.

One of the key strengths of fintech infrastructure in Côte d'Ivoire is its widespread accessibility, facilitated by the extensive coverage of mobile networks and the proliferation of mobile phone ownership. With over 35 million mobile subscriptions and a mobile penetration rate exceeding 100% as of 2021, according to the World Bank, mobile phones have become ubiquitous tools for accessing financial services and conducting transactions across the country. This high level of mobile connectivity has played a crucial role in driving fintech adoption and promoting financial inclusion, particularly among underserved populations in rural and remote areas.

Moreover, the regulatory framework governing fintech activities in Côte d'Ivoire has played a pivotal role in shaping the infrastructure and access to financial services. The Central Bank of West African States (BCEAO) has established clear guidelines and regulations governing electronic money institutions (EMIs) and mobile money operators, ensuring the stability, integrity, and security of the financial system. These regulations outline requirements for licensing, capital adequacy, risk management, and consumer protection, providing a framework for fintech players to operate within.

An example that illustrates the importance of fintech infrastructure and access in Côte d'Ivoire is the role of mobile money in facilitating financial transactions during the COVID-19 pandemic. With lockdown measures and restrictions on movement in place to curb the spread of the virus, mobile money platforms emerged as lifelines for millions of Ivorians, enabling them to send and receive money, pay bills, and access essential goods and services without the need for physical contact. This demonstrated the resilience and adaptability of fintech infrastructure in providing essential financial services during times of crisis.

However, despite the progress made in expanding fintech infrastructure and access in Côte d'Ivoire, challenges remain, particularly in rural and underserved areas where internet connectivity and financial literacy levels may be lower. Additionally, interoperability between different mobile money platforms and traditional banking systems remains a key issue, hindering the seamless transfer of funds and transactions across different channels. Efforts to address these challenges and promote inclusivity in fintech adoption are crucial for ensuring that all segments of the population can benefit from the opportunities afforded by digital finance.

Fintech infrastructure and access in Côte d'Ivoire have evolved significantly in recent years, driven by the widespread availability of mobile phones, regulatory reforms, and industry collaborations. The accessibility and resilience of mobile money platforms have played a pivotal role in promoting financial inclusion and empowering individuals and businesses to participate in the formal economy. Moving forward, stakeholders must continue to invest in infrastructure development, regulatory compliance, and consumer education to further enhance the accessibility and inclusivity of fintech services in Côte d'Ivoire.

Regulatory Framework for Fintech and Counterterrorism

The regulatory framework governing fintech activities in Côte d'Ivoire is critical for promoting innovation, ensuring financial stability, and mitigating risks, including those related to terrorism financing. The Central Bank of West African States (BCEAO) plays a central role in overseeing and regulating fintech activities in member countries, including Côte d'Ivoire. The BCEAO has issued comprehensive regulations and guidelines governing electronic money institutions (EMIs), mobile money operators, and other fintech service providers, aimed at safeguarding the integrity and security of the financial system.

One of the key components of the regulatory framework is the requirement for licensing and authorization of fintech operators by the BCEAO. Fintech companies offering electronic money services, mobile money platforms, and digital payment solutions are subject to stringent licensing requirements, including capital adequacy, operational infrastructure, risk management, and compliance with anti-money laundering (AML) and counterterrorism financing (CTF) regulations. For example, mobile money operators in Côte d'Ivoire are required to obtain a license from the BCEAO and comply with strict AML/CFT measures, such as customer due diligence (CDD), transaction monitoring, and reporting of suspicious activities.

Moreover, the regulatory framework includes provisions for consumer protection and financial inclusion, ensuring that fintech services are accessible, affordable, and safe for users. The BCEAO has established guidelines for customer identification, transaction limits, dispute resolution, and transparency of fees to enhance consumer trust and confidence in fintech platforms. These regulations aim to strike a balance between fostering innovation and protecting the interests of consumers, particularly vulnerable populations who may be at risk of financial exploitation or fraud.

An example that highlights the importance of the regulatory framework for fintech and counterterrorism in Côte d'Ivoire is the case of regulatory reforms introduced in response to emerging risks and threats. In recent years, the Ivorian government has strengthened its AML/CFT regime by enacting laws, regulations, and directives aimed at enhancing the detection and prevention of illicit financial activities, including terrorism financing. For instance, Law No. 2016-992 on combating money laundering and terrorism financing provides a comprehensive legal framework for identifying, investigating, and prosecuting individuals and entities involved in illicit financial activities, including those using fintech platforms.

However, while the regulatory framework for fintech in Côte d'Ivoire is robust, challenges remain in effectively addressing terrorism financing risks within the digital finance ecosystem. The rapid pace of technological innovation and the evolving nature of financial crimes present ongoing challenges for regulators and law enforcement agencies. Additionally, the cross-border nature of fintech transactions and the anonymity afforded by digital platforms pose challenges for monitoring and surveillance efforts.

The regulatory framework for fintech and counterterrorism in Côte d'Ivoire plays a crucial role in promoting financial integrity, protecting consumers, and mitigating risks to national security. While significant progress has been made in strengthening regulations and enhancing compliance measures, ongoing efforts are needed to address emerging threats and vulnerabilities within the fintech ecosystem. Collaboration between government agencies, regulatory authorities, financial institutions, and technology providers is essential for developing effective strategies to combat terrorism financing while fostering innovation and financial inclusion in Côte d'Ivoire.

Compliance Requirements for Fintech Operators

In Côte d'Ivoire, fintech operators are subject to stringent compliance requirements aimed at ensuring the integrity, security, and stability of the financial system, as well as mitigating risks such as money laundering and terrorism financing. These compliance requirements are set forth by regulatory authorities such as the Central Bank of West African States (BCEAO) and are enforced through a combination of regulations, directives, and supervisory mechanisms.

One of the primary compliance requirements for fintech operators is obtaining proper licensing and authorization from the regulatory authorities. Fintech companies offering electronic money services, mobile money platforms, digital payment solutions, and other financial services are required to apply for and obtain licenses from the BCEAO before commencing operations. These licenses are granted based on criteria such as capital adequacy, operational infrastructure, risk management capabilities, and compliance with AML/CFT regulations. For example, mobile money operators in Côte d'Ivoire must demonstrate compliance with strict AML/CFT measures, including customer due diligence (CDD), transaction monitoring, and reporting of suspicious activities, as part of their licensing requirements.

Furthermore, fintech operators are required to adhere to specific regulatory requirements related to customer identification and verification procedures. Under the regulatory framework, fintech companies must implement robust Know Your Customer (KYC) and Customer Due Diligence (CDD) processes to verify the identity of their customers, assess their risk profiles, and monitor their transactions for suspicious activities. These requirements are essential for mitigating the risk of fraud, money laundering, and terrorism financing, as they enable fintech operators to identify and mitigate potential risks associated with their customers' activities.

In addition to customer identification and verification, fintech operators are also required to implement adequate risk management and compliance programs to ensure adherence to regulatory requirements and industry best practices. This includes establishing internal controls, policies, and procedures to detect, prevent, and report financial crimes such as money laundering and terrorism financing. Fintech companies are also expected to conduct regular risk assessments, internal audits, and training programs to ensure that their staff are aware of their compliance obligations and equipped to identify and address potential risks effectively.

An example that illustrates the importance of compliance requirements for fintech operators in Côte d'Ivoire is the case of regulatory enforcement actions taken against non-compliant entities. In recent years, regulatory authorities in Côte d'Ivoire have taken proactive measures to enforce compliance with AML/CFT regulations and sanction fintech operators found to be in violation of regulatory requirements. For instance, the BCEAO has imposed fines, penalties, and license revocations on mobile money operators and electronic money institutions found to have deficiencies in their compliance programs or inadequate controls for detecting and preventing financial crimes.

However, while compliance requirements are essential for safeguarding the integrity of the financial system and mitigating risks, they also pose challenges for fintech operators, particularly smaller startups and innovators with limited resources and expertise in regulatory compliance. Compliance costs, regulatory complexity, and administrative burdens can act as barriers to entry for new entrants and stifle innovation in the fintech sector. Therefore, it is crucial for regulators to strike a balance between regulatory oversight and fostering innovation by providing clear guidance, support, and incentives for fintech operators to comply with regulatory requirements effectively.

Compliance requirements for fintech operators in Côte d'Ivoire play a crucial role in ensuring the integrity, security, and stability of the financial system, as well as mitigating risks such as money laundering and terrorism financing. While regulatory compliance is essential for safeguarding the interests of consumers and maintaining trust in financial institutions, regulators must also be mindful of the potential impact of compliance requirements on innovation and competition in the fintech sector. Therefore, a collaborative approach between regulators, fintech operators, and other stakeholders is necessary to develop and implement effective compliance frameworks that promote both regulatory compliance and innovation in Côte d'Ivoire's fintech ecosystem.

Anti-Money Laundering (AML) and Counterterrorism Financing (CTF) Regulations

In Côte d'Ivoire, like in many countries around the world, robust anti-money laundering (AML) and counterterrorism financing (CTF) regulations are crucial for safeguarding the integrity of the financial system and mitigating risks associated with illicit financial activities. These regulations are designed to detect, prevent, and deter money laundering, terrorist financing, and other financial crimes by imposing obligations on financial institutions, including fintech operators, to implement comprehensive compliance programs and reporting mechanisms.

The regulatory framework for AML and CTF in Côte d'Ivoire is primarily governed by legislation such as Law No. 2016-992 on combating money laundering and terrorism financing, as well as regulations issued by the Central Bank of West African States (BCEAO) and other relevant authorities. These regulations establish clear requirements for customer due diligence (CDD), transaction monitoring, suspicious activity reporting, and record-keeping, among other obligations, to ensure that financial institutions have robust systems and controls in place to identify and mitigate risks of money laundering and terrorism financing.

For example, under the AML/CTF regulations in Côte d'Ivoire, financial institutions, including fintech operators, are required to conduct thorough customer due diligence (CDD) procedures to verify the identity of their customers, assess their risk profiles, and monitor their transactions for suspicious activities. This includes collecting and verifying customer identification documents, screening customers against sanctions lists and politically exposed persons (PEP) databases, and monitoring transactions for red flags indicative of money laundering or terrorism financing activities.

Moreover, fintech operators in Côte d'Ivoire are also required to establish robust transaction monitoring and reporting mechanisms to detect and report suspicious activities to the relevant authorities. This includes implementing automated systems and algorithms to analyze transaction patterns, identify anomalies, and generate alerts for further investigation. Fintech operators are also obligated to maintain comprehensive records of their customers, transactions, and compliance activities, which can be used for audit, oversight, and law enforcement purposes.

An example that highlights the importance of AML/CTF regulations in Côte d'Ivoire is the case of regulatory enforcement actions taken against non-compliant financial institutions. In recent years, regulatory authorities in Côte d'Ivoire, including the BCEAO and the Ministry of Economy and Finance, have conducted inspections, audits, and investigations to assess compliance with AML/CTF regulations and sanction institutions found to violate regulatory requirements. This has resulted in fines, penalties, license revocations, and other enforcement actions against financial institutions that have failed to implement adequate AML/CTF controls or report suspicious activities effectively.

However, while AML/CTF regulations play a crucial role in combating financial crimes, including money laundering and terrorism financing, they also pose challenges for fintech operators, particularly smaller startups and innovators with limited resources and expertise in regulatory compliance. Compliance costs, regulatory complexity, and administrative burdens can act as barriers to entry for new entrants and stifle innovation in the fintech sector. Therefore, regulators need to provide clear guidance, support, and training to fintech operators to help them comply with AML/CTF regulations effectively while fostering innovation and competition in the financial sector.

The AML/CTF regulations are essential for maintaining the integrity, security, and stability of the financial system in Côte d'Ivoire and mitigating risks associated with money laundering and terrorism financing. While compliance with these regulations imposes obligations on fintech operators, it is crucial for regulators to strike a balance between regulatory oversight and fostering innovation by providing guidance, support, and incentives for compliance. By working collaboratively with regulators, financial institutions, and other stakeholders, fintech operators can play a proactive role in combating financial crimes and promoting a safe and secure financial ecosystem in Côte d'Ivoire.

Vulnerabilities and Risks in the Ivorian Fintech Ecosystem

Threat Landscape Analysis

Understanding the threat landscape is critical for fintech operators and regulatory authorities in Côte d'Ivoire to identify and mitigate risks associated with money laundering, terrorism financing, and other financial crimes. The evolving nature of technology and the increasing digitization of financial services have introduced new vulnerabilities and challenges that require a proactive and adaptive approach to risk management.

One of the key threats facing fintech operators in Côte d'Ivoire is the risk of cyberattacks and data breaches. As fintech platforms rely on digital infrastructure and online transactions, they are susceptible to hacking attempts, malware infections, and other cyber threats that can compromise the security and confidentiality of customer data. For example, phishing attacks targeting mobile money users in Côte d'Ivoire have been reported, where fraudsters attempt to deceive individuals into disclosing their account credentials or personal information through fake messages or websites.

Moreover, fintech operators also face risks related to money laundering and terrorism financing, whereby illicit actors exploit digital platforms to launder proceeds from criminal activities or fund terrorist organizations. The anonymity and convenience offered by fintech services, such as mobile money and digital currencies, can be leveraged by criminals to transfer funds across borders quickly and discreetly. For instance, there have been cases of mobile money agents in Côte d'Ivoire being used as conduits for illicit financial transactions, highlighting the vulnerabilities within the fintech ecosystem.

Another threat to fintech operators in Côte d'Ivoire is the risk of insider abuse and fraud, where employees or trusted individuals misuse their access to sensitive information or systems for personal gain or malicious purposes. Insider threats can range from unauthorized access to customer data to collusion with external parties to facilitate fraudulent transactions. For example, there have been instances of insider fraud involving employees of financial institutions and fintech companies in Côte d'Ivoire, leading to financial losses and reputational damage.

Furthermore, the transnational nature of fintech transactions and the interconnectedness of the global financial system pose challenges for regulatory authorities in Côte d'Ivoire to monitor and enforce compliance with AML/CFT regulations effectively. Criminal organizations and terrorist groups exploit regulatory gaps and jurisdictional differences to launder money and finance illicit activities across borders, making it difficult for authorities to track and disrupt their operations. For instance, cross-border remittances and digital currency transactions present unique challenges for AML/CFT compliance due to the anonymity and decentralized nature of these transactions.

In response to these threats, fintech operators and regulatory authorities in Côte d'Ivoire must adopt a risk-based approach to compliance and implement robust controls and safeguards to detect and prevent financial crimes effectively. This includes investing in cybersecurity measures, enhancing customer due diligence processes, conducting regular risk assessments, and fostering collaboration and information sharing among stakeholders. By staying vigilant and proactive in addressing emerging threats, fintech operators and regulatory authorities can safeguard the integrity and stability of the financial system and promote trust and confidence in digital financial services in Côte d'Ivoire.

Case Studies of Fintech-Enabled Terrorism Financing

Examining real-world case studies of fintech-enabled terrorism financing provides valuable insights into the methods, challenges, and implications of illicit financial activities in the digital age. While specific cases of terrorism financing through fintech platforms may be limited in Côte d'Ivoire, analyzing global examples can shed light on potential risks and vulnerabilities within the Ivorian financial ecosystem.

One notable case is the use of cryptocurrencies by terrorist organizations to raise funds and finance their operations. Cryptocurrencies such as Bitcoin offer anonymity, decentralization, and cross-border transferability, making them attractive tools for terrorist groups seeking to evade traditional financial controls and sanctions. For example, in 2019, the U.S. Department of Justice (DOJ) charged two individuals with using Bitcoin and other cryptocurrencies to launder money on behalf of the terrorist group Hamas. The individuals allegedly operated a network of unlicensed money-transmitting businesses that facilitated the transfer of funds to Hamas operatives in Gaza, highlighting the challenges of regulating cryptocurrency transactions and detecting illicit activities.

Additionally, mobile money platforms have been exploited by criminal networks and terrorist groups to transfer funds and finance illicit activities in conflict-affected regions. For instance, in the Lake Chad Basin region of West Africa, terrorist organizations such as Boko Haram have reportedly used mobile money services to collect ransom payments, extort businesses, and finance their insurgency. The ease of use, accessibility, and anonymity offered by mobile money platforms make them attractive channels for terrorist financing, particularly in areas with limited banking infrastructure and regulatory oversight.

Furthermore, social media and online crowdfunding platforms have emerged as avenues for terrorist organizations to solicit donations and raise funds from sympathizers and supporters worldwide. While these platforms are not inherently fintech in nature, they facilitate financial transactions and fundraising activities that can be leveraged for terrorism financing purposes. For example, in 2019, the U.S. Treasury Department designated a Lebanese-based social media company as a facilitator of terrorism financing for its role in promoting and facilitating fundraising campaigns for Hezbollah, a designated terrorist organization. This case underscores the challenges of regulating online fundraising activities and disrupting terrorist financing networks operating in cyberspace.

While these case studies highlight the evolving threats and challenges posed by fintech-enabled terrorism financing, it is essential to recognize that the vast majority of fintech transactions are legitimate and contribute to economic growth and financial inclusion. Therefore, policymakers and regulatory authorities in Côte d'Ivoire must strike a balance between fostering innovation and addressing the risks associated with fintech-enabled financial crimes. This requires implementing targeted regulatory measures, enhancing compliance and oversight mechanisms, and fostering collaboration with industry stakeholders and international partners to combat terrorism financing effectively while promoting the benefits of digital financial services. By learning from global case studies and adapting best practices to the Ivorian context, stakeholders can strengthen the resilience of the fintech sector and safeguard the integrity of the financial system against emerging threats and vulnerabilities.

Insider Threats and Social Engineering Attacks

Insider threats and social engineering attacks pose significant risks to the security and integrity of fintech operations in Côte d'Ivoire, highlighting the importance of robust cybersecurity measures and employee awareness training. Insider threats occur when individuals with authorized access to sensitive information or systems misuse their privileges for personal gain, malicious purposes, or unintentional negligence. This can include employees, contractors, or trusted third parties who exploit vulnerabilities within the organization's security controls to commit fraud, steal data, or compromise systems.

One example of insider threats in the fintech sector is the case of employee misconduct or fraud within financial institutions and fintech companies. In Côte d'Ivoire and globally, there have been instances where employees with access to sensitive customer information or transactional data have abused their positions to engage in fraudulent activities, such as unauthorized transfers, identity theft, or data breaches. For instance, in 2018, a former employee of a major U.S. fintech company was charged with stealing millions of dollars from customer accounts by exploiting vulnerabilities in the company's internal systems and processes.

Social engineering attacks, on the other hand, involve the manipulation of individuals through psychological tactics to trick them into divulging confidential information, providing access to sensitive systems, or performing unauthorized actions. These attacks often exploit human vulnerabilities, such as trust, curiosity, or fear, to deceive victims into taking actions that compromise security. Common social engineering techniques include phishing emails, pretexting phone calls, and impersonation scams, which aim to exploit unsuspecting individuals' trust and familiarity with legitimate institutions or individuals.

In Côte d'Ivoire, fintech users and employees are increasingly targeted by social engineering attacks aimed at stealing personal information, login credentials, or financial assets. For example, phishing emails impersonating mobile money providers or financial institutions may lure users into clicking malicious links, downloading malware-infected attachments, or disclosing their account credentials under pretenses. Similarly, pretexting phone calls from fraudsters posing as customer service representatives may trick individuals into revealing sensitive information or authorizing fraudulent transactions.

The implications of insider threats and social engineering attacks extend beyond financial losses to include reputational damage, regulatory sanctions, and erosion of customer trust. A successful insider attack or social engineering scheme can compromise sensitive data, disrupt operations, and undermine the integrity of the fintech ecosystem, impacting both individuals and businesses. Moreover, the interconnected nature of fintech platforms and the rapid proliferation of digital services amplify the potential impact of insider threats and social engineering attacks, necessitating proactive measures to mitigate risks and protect against emerging threats.

To address insider threats and social engineering attacks effectively, fintech operators in Côte d'Ivoire must implement a multi-layered approach to cybersecurity that combines technical controls, employee training, and incident response capabilities. This includes implementing access controls, encryption, and monitoring tools to detect and prevent unauthorized access or misuse of sensitive data. Additionally, employee awareness training programs can educate staff about the risks of social engineering attacks and guide how to identify and respond to suspicious activities. By fostering a culture of security awareness and resilience, fintech operators can strengthen their defenses against insider threats and social engineering attacks and mitigate the risks posed by malicious actors within and outside the organization.

Counterterrorism Strategies and Policy Responses

Government Initiatives and Stakeholder Collaboration

Government initiatives and stakeholder collaboration play a crucial role in addressing the security challenges facing the fintech sector in Côte d'Ivoire, fostering a collaborative ecosystem for innovation, regulation, and risk management. Recognizing the importance of cybersecurity and financial integrity, the Ivorian government has taken proactive measures to strengthen the regulatory framework, promote industry best practices, and enhance collaboration among stakeholders to mitigate risks and protect consumers.

One key government initiative in Côte d'Ivoire is the establishment of regulatory frameworks and supervisory mechanisms to oversee fintech activities and ensure compliance with relevant laws and regulations. The Central Bank of West African States (BCEAO) plays a central role in regulating fintech operations in member countries, including Côte d'Ivoire, by issuing guidelines, directives, and regulations governing electronic money institutions (EMIs), mobile money operators, and digital payment providers. For example, the BCEAO has issued regulations requiring fintech operators to implement robust AML/CFT controls, conduct customer due diligence, and report suspicious activities to regulatory authorities.

Moreover, the Ivorian government has launched initiatives to promote stakeholder collaboration and information sharing to address cybersecurity threats and financial crimes effectively. For instance, the Ministry of Digital Economy and Post collaborates with industry associations, financial institutions, technology providers, and law enforcement agencies to share intelligence, best practices, and resources for combating cyber threats and protecting consumers. Similarly, the Ivorian Fintech Association (Fintech CI) serves as a platform for fintech startups, regulators, and investors to collaborate on initiatives related to cybersecurity, regulatory compliance, and market development.

Furthermore, international collaboration and partnerships are essential for addressing transnational cybersecurity threats and financial crimes that transcend borders. Côte d'Ivoire participates in regional and international forums, such as the West African Economic and Monetary Union (WAEMU), the Inter-Governmental Action Group against Money Laundering in West Africa (GIABA), and the Financial Action Task Force (FATF), to exchange information, coordinate regulatory efforts, and enhance capacity-building initiatives to combat money laundering, terrorism financing, and cybercrimes. For example, Côte d'Ivoire underwent a mutual evaluation process by GIABA in 2019 to assess its AML/CFT regime and identify areas for improvement, demonstrating the government's commitment to international cooperation and compliance with global standards.

However, while government initiatives and stakeholder collaboration are essential for addressing security challenges in the fintech sector, several areas require critical analysis and improvement. One challenge is the need for greater coordination and alignment among regulatory authorities, industry associations, and law enforcement agencies to ensure a cohesive and consistent approach to cybersecurity and financial crime prevention. Fragmentation and overlapping responsibilities between government agencies and regulatory bodies may hinder effective collaboration and information sharing, leading to gaps in oversight and enforcement.

Additionally, there is a need for ongoing capacity-building initiatives to enhance the cybersecurity skills and expertise of regulatory authorities, financial institutions, and fintech operators in Côte d'Ivoire. Investing in training programs, workshops, and certifications can empower stakeholders with the knowledge and tools needed to identify, assess, and mitigate cybersecurity risks effectively. Furthermore, raising public awareness and promoting cybersecurity hygiene among consumers is essential for building resilience against social engineering attacks, phishing scams, and other cyber threats targeting individuals and businesses.

Government initiatives and stakeholder collaboration are essential pillars of cybersecurity and financial crime prevention in the fintech sector in Côte d'Ivoire. By fostering a collaborative ecosystem that promotes regulatory compliance, information sharing, and capacity building, stakeholders can work together to mitigate risks, protect consumers, and promote trust and confidence in digital financial services. However, continued efforts are needed to address regulatory challenges, enhance coordination, and build cybersecurity resilience to effectively combat emerging threats and safeguard the integrity of the fintech ecosystem in Côte d'Ivoire.

Enhancing Regulatory Enforcement and Oversight

Regulatory enforcement and oversight are critical components of ensuring the integrity, stability, and security of the fintech sector in Côte d'Ivoire. Effective enforcement mechanisms and robust oversight frameworks are essential for holding fintech operators accountable, detecting regulatory violations, and mitigating risks associated with financial crimes, including money laundering, terrorism financing, and fraud.

One aspect of enhancing regulatory enforcement and oversight involves strengthening the capacity and authority of regulatory authorities to enforce compliance with existing regulations and laws governing the fintech sector. In Côte d'Ivoire, the Central Bank of West African States (BCEAO) plays a central role in regulating and supervising fintech activities, issuing licenses, and setting prudential standards for electronic money institutions (EMIs), mobile money operators, and other financial service providers. However, regulatory authorities may face challenges in enforcing compliance due to resource constraints, limited expertise, and evolving threats in the digital landscape.

To address these challenges, regulators in Côte d'Ivoire can enhance regulatory enforcement and oversight by investing in technology-enabled supervisory tools, conducting regular inspections and audits, and imposing penalties and sanctions on non-compliant operators. For example, regulators can leverage data analytics, artificial intelligence, and machine learning algorithms to monitor fintech transactions, detect suspicious activities, and identify patterns indicative of money laundering or terrorism financing. By leveraging technology-driven approaches, regulators can enhance their surveillance capabilities, improve risk assessment accuracy, and identify emerging threats more effectively.

Moreover, regulatory authorities can collaborate with industry stakeholders, international partners, and law enforcement agencies to share information, coordinate enforcement actions, and conduct joint investigations into financial crimes. Collaborative initiatives such as information-sharing networks, task forces, and regulatory sandboxes can facilitate cooperation among regulators, fintech operators, and other stakeholders, enabling more agile responses to emerging risks and challenges. For instance, the West African Economic and Monetary Union (WAEMU) provides a platform for member countries, including Côte d'Ivoire, to collaborate on regulatory harmonization, capacity building, and cross-border enforcement efforts to combat money laundering and terrorism financing.

However, while enhancing regulatory enforcement and oversight is essential for maintaining financial integrity and consumer protection, it is crucial to strike a balance between regulatory compliance and fostering innovation in the fintech sector. Excessive regulatory burden, overzealous enforcement, and regulatory uncertainty can stifle innovation, deter investment, and impede the growth of the fintech ecosystem. Therefore, regulators in Côte d'Ivoire must adopt a risk-based approach to supervision, focusing on high-risk activities and entities while providing flexibility and support for compliant operators to innovate and expand their services.

Additionally, regulatory authorities should engage in proactive dialogue with industry stakeholders to solicit feedback, address concerns, and co-create regulatory solutions that balance regulatory objectives with industry realities. Regulatory sandboxes, pilot programs, and regulatory consultations can provide fintech operators with a safe space to test innovative products and services under regulatory supervision, enabling regulators to assess risks, gather data, and tailor regulatory requirements accordingly.

Enhancing regulatory enforcement and oversight is essential for ensuring the integrity, stability, and security of the fintech sector in Côte d'Ivoire. By strengthening regulatory capacity, leveraging technology-enabled supervisory tools, and fostering collaboration among stakeholders, regulators can enhance their ability to detect and deter financial crimes, protect consumers, and promote a sound and resilient fintech ecosystem. However, regulators must strike a balance between regulatory compliance and innovation, ensuring that regulatory measures are proportionate, risk-based, and supportive of fintech innovation and growth in Côte d'Ivoire.

Promoting Public Awareness and Education

Promoting public awareness and education is a crucial aspect of fostering a secure and resilient fintech ecosystem in Côte d'Ivoire. Educating consumers, businesses, and other stakeholders about the risks and opportunities associated with fintech services is essential for empowering them to make informed decisions, protect themselves against cyber threats, and utilize digital financial services safely and responsibly.

One strategy for promoting public awareness and education is through targeted outreach campaigns and educational initiatives led by government agencies, industry associations, and financial institutions. These campaigns can raise awareness about common cyber threats, such as phishing scams, identity theft, and fraud, and provide practical tips and best practices for safeguarding personal and financial information. For example, the Ivorian government could collaborate with fintech companies and consumer advocacy groups to develop educational materials, workshops, and online resources that educate consumers about the risks of sharing sensitive information online and the importance of using secure passwords, enabling two-factor authentication, and regularly updating software and antivirus programs.

Furthermore, financial literacy programs and workshops can help individuals and businesses understand how fintech services work, their rights and responsibilities as users, and how to navigate digital financial platforms effectively. For instance, the Central Bank of West African States (BCEAO) could organize workshops and seminars in collaboration with local financial institutions and community organizations to educate consumers about the benefits of mobile money, digital payments, and other fintech innovations, as well as how to access and use these services securely.

Moreover, promoting public awareness and education also involves addressing the digital divide and ensuring that underserved and marginalized communities have access to information and resources to participate in the digital economy safely and equitably. This may involve partnering with community organizations, non-profit groups, and telecommunications providers to expand internet access, provide digital skills training, and promote financial inclusion initiatives targeted at vulnerable populations, such as women, youth, and rural communities. For example, fintech companies like M-Pesa have launched initiatives to promote financial literacy and entrepreneurship among women in Africa, providing training and support to help women access and use mobile money services to improve their economic livelihoods.

However, while promoting public awareness and education is essential for empowering consumers and businesses to navigate the fintech landscape safely, it is important to critically assess the effectiveness of these initiatives and address any gaps or challenges in reaching target audiences. Factors such as language barriers, literacy levels, and digital literacy skills may impact the accessibility and effectiveness of educational materials and programs, particularly in underserved communities. Therefore, stakeholders need to adopt a culturally sensitive and inclusive approach to public awareness and education, tailoring messages and delivery methods to the needs and preferences of diverse audiences.

Promoting public awareness and education is a vital component of building a secure and inclusive fintech ecosystem in Côte d'Ivoire. By raising awareness about cyber threats, promoting financial literacy, and addressing barriers to access and participation, stakeholders can empower individuals and communities to take advantage of fintech innovations safely and responsibly. However, ongoing evaluation and adaptation of educational initiatives are necessary to ensure their relevance, effectiveness, and impact in addressing the evolving needs and challenges of fintech users in Côte d'Ivoire.

Recommendations for Strengthening Fintech Security and Counterterrorism Measures

Policy Implications and Strategic Interventions

The rapid growth of the fintech sector in Côte d'Ivoire presents policymakers with both opportunities and challenges that require strategic interventions to maximize the benefits of innovation while mitigating risks and safeguarding financial stability. Policy implications and strategic interventions encompass a wide range of regulatory, legislative, and institutional measures aimed at creating an enabling environment for fintech innovation, enhancing consumer protection, and addressing emerging threats in the digital financial ecosystem.

One key policy implication is the need for agile and adaptive regulatory frameworks that can keep pace with technological advancements and evolving risks in the fintech sector. Policymakers must strike a balance between promoting innovation and protecting consumers by designing regulations that are technology-neutral, principles-based, and proportionate to the risks posed by fintech activities. For example, regulators could adopt a regulatory sandbox approach to encourage experimentation and innovation in a controlled environment while providing regulatory relief and support for compliant fintech startups to test new products and services.

Moreover, policymakers must prioritize consumer protection measures to ensure that fintech services are safe, transparent, and accessible to all segments of society. This may involve implementing robust licensing and registration requirements for fintech operators, enforcing compliance with data protection and privacy laws, and establishing dispute resolution mechanisms to address consumer complaints and grievances. For instance, the Ivorian government could establish a dedicated consumer protection agency or ombudsman to oversee fintech-related complaints and enforce consumer rights following existing laws and regulations.

Furthermore, policymakers must address the cybersecurity and operational resilience challenges facing the fintech sector by promoting industry-wide standards, best practices, and collaborative initiatives. This may include developing cybersecurity guidelines, conducting cybersecurity audits and assessments, and establishing information-sharing platforms to facilitate collaboration among regulators, industry stakeholders, and law enforcement agencies. For example, the Ivorian government could establish a national cybersecurity center or task force to coordinate cyber defense efforts, share threat intelligence, and respond to cyber incidents affecting the fintech sector.

Additionally, policymakers must consider the broader economic and social implications of fintech innovation, including its impact on financial inclusion, economic development, and job creation. Strategic interventions such as promoting digital literacy, supporting entrepreneurship, and fostering partnerships between fintech startups and traditional financial institutions can help maximize the socio-economic benefits of fintech while mitigating potential risks, such as job displacement and income inequality. For instance, the Ivorian government could launch initiatives to provide training and mentorship to aspiring fintech entrepreneurs, create incentives for fintech investment and innovation, and promote collaboration between fintech startups and local SMEs to drive inclusive growth and innovation.

However, while policy interventions are essential for shaping the future of the fintech sector in Côte d'Ivoire, it is crucial to adopt a holistic and collaborative approach that engages stakeholders from across the public and private sectors. Policymakers must consult with industry stakeholders, civil society organizations, academia, and international partners to develop evidence-based policies that reflect the diverse needs and interests of the fintech ecosystem. Moreover, policymakers must prioritize regulatory coherence, coordination, and harmonization at the regional and international levels to ensure that regulatory frameworks are consistent, interoperable, and conducive to cross-border fintech activities.

Policy implications and strategic interventions are critical for fostering a dynamic, inclusive, and resilient fintech ecosystem in Côte d'Ivoire. By adopting a forward-thinking regulatory approach, prioritizing consumer protection, promoting cybersecurity resilience, and maximizing the socio-economic benefits of fintech innovation, policymakers can create an enabling environment for sustainable fintech growth and innovation while mitigating risks and safeguarding financial stability. However, achieving these objectives requires proactive engagement, collaboration, and coordination among all stakeholders to address the complex challenges and opportunities facing the fintech sector in Côte d'Ivoire and beyond.

Regulatory Reforms and Capacity Building Initiatives

Regulatory reforms and capacity-building initiatives are essential components of creating a conducive regulatory environment and building institutional resilience in the fintech sector of Côte d'Ivoire. As the fintech landscape evolves rapidly, policymakers must continuously review and update regulatory frameworks to accommodate technological advancements, address emerging risks, and promote innovation while ensuring financial stability and consumer protection.

One key aspect of regulatory reforms is the development of clear and comprehensive regulatory frameworks that provide certainty, clarity, and stability for fintech operators and investors. Regulatory clarity is essential for fostering investor confidence, attracting capital investment, and promoting fintech innovation in Côte d'Ivoire. For example, the Central Bank of West African States (BCEAO) could issue guidelines and directives that clarify the licensing requirements, regulatory obligations, and permissible activities for fintech operators, such as electronic money institutions (EMIs), payment service providers, and digital asset exchanges.

Moreover, regulatory reforms should prioritize risk-based supervision and proportionate regulation to accommodate the diverse nature and scale of fintech activities. Rather than adopting a one-size-fits-all approach, regulators should tailor regulatory requirements to the specific risks posed by fintech activities, taking into account factors such as the size, complexity, and systemic importance of fintech operators. For instance, regulators could implement tiered licensing regimes that impose lighter regulatory requirements on small fintech startups and innovative ventures while subjecting larger, more systemically important operators to stricter oversight and supervision.

Furthermore, capacity-building initiatives are essential for enhancing the regulatory capacity and expertise of supervisory authorities, law enforcement agencies, and other relevant stakeholders responsible for overseeing the fintech sector. Investing in training programs, workshops, and technical assistance can empower regulators with the knowledge, skills, and tools needed to assess and mitigate risks associated with fintech activities effectively. For example, the Ivorian government could collaborate with international organizations, such as the International Monetary Fund (IMF) or the World Bank, to provide technical assistance and capacity-building support for regulatory agencies responsible for supervising the fintech sector.

Additionally, capacity-building initiatives should extend beyond regulatory authorities to encompass fintech operators, industry associations, academia, and other stakeholders involved in the fintech ecosystem. By providing training and guidance on regulatory compliance, risk management, and best practices, capacity-building initiatives can help fintech operators navigate regulatory requirements, build internal controls, and foster a culture of compliance and accountability. For instance, industry associations like Fintech CI could organize training workshops and certification programs to educate fintech startups and entrepreneurs about regulatory obligations, industry standards, and market trends.

However, while regulatory reforms and capacity-building initiatives are essential for strengthening the regulatory environment and building institutional capacity in the fintech sector, it is important to critically assess the effectiveness and impact of these interventions. Policymakers must monitor and evaluate the implementation of regulatory reforms, identify gaps and shortcomings in regulatory frameworks, and adapt policies and strategies as needed to address emerging challenges and opportunities in the fintech landscape. Moreover, policymakers should foster collaboration and dialogue with industry stakeholders, consumer advocates, and international partners to ensure that regulatory reforms are balanced, inclusive, and responsive to the evolving needs and dynamics of the fintech ecosystem in Côte d'Ivoire.

Regulatory reforms and capacity-building initiatives are indispensable for creating a robust, inclusive, and sustainable regulatory framework for the fintech sector in Côte d'Ivoire. By adopting a forward-looking approach to regulation, promoting regulatory clarity and proportionality, and investing in regulatory capacity and expertise, policymakers can create an enabling environment for fintech innovation, protect consumers, and ensure financial stability in the digital era. However, achieving these objectives requires continued commitment, collaboration, and adaptability from all stakeholders to navigate the complex and evolving challenges of the fintech landscape effectively.

Technological Solutions and Best Practices

Technological solutions and best practices play a pivotal role in bolstering the security, efficiency, and resilience of the fintech sector in Côte d'Ivoire. As fintech innovations continue to disrupt traditional financial services, leveraging advanced technologies and adopting industry best practices are essential for mitigating risks, enhancing operational efficiency, and ensuring a seamless user experience.

One critical aspect of technological solutions in fintech is cybersecurity measures, which are paramount for safeguarding sensitive data, preventing cyberattacks, and maintaining trust in digital financial services. Fintech operators can deploy a range of cybersecurity technologies, such as encryption, multi-factor authentication, and intrusion detection systems, to protect against unauthorized access, data breaches, and other cyber threats. For example, fintech companies like Ecobank in Côte d'Ivoire have invested in advanced encryption technologies and robust authentication mechanisms to secure mobile banking and digital payment transactions, ensuring the confidentiality and integrity of customer data.

Moreover, adopting industry best practices such as adherence to international cybersecurity standards, conducting regular security audits and penetration testing, and implementing incident response plans are essential for building resilience against cyber threats. For instance, fintech startups and financial institutions in Côte d'Ivoire can align their cybersecurity practices with globally recognized frameworks such as the ISO/IEC 27001 standard or the NIST Cybersecurity Framework to enhance their cybersecurity posture and demonstrate their commitment to security to customers, partners, and regulators.

Additionally, technological solutions can drive operational efficiency and innovation in the fintech sector by automating processes, streamlining workflows, and optimizing resource allocation. For example, fintech companies in Côte d'Ivoire can leverage artificial intelligence (AI) and machine learning algorithms to automate customer onboarding, credit scoring, and fraud detection processes, reducing manual errors, improving accuracy, and enhancing the overall customer experience. By harnessing the power of data analytics and predictive modeling, fintech operators can gain actionable insights into customer behavior, market trends, and risk profiles, enabling them to make data-driven decisions and develop tailored products and services that meet the evolving needs of consumers.

Furthermore, technological solutions such as distributed ledger technology (DLT) and blockchain can enhance transparency, traceability, and security in financial transactions, particularly in areas such as remittances, cross-border payments, and supply chain finance. For instance, blockchain-based platforms like RippleNet enable real-time, low-cost cross-border payments between financial institutions, reducing settlement times and transaction costs while enhancing transparency and auditability. Similarly, fintech startups like Koosmik in Côte d'Ivoire are leveraging blockchain technology to facilitate peer-to-peer payments and remittances, providing users with a secure, efficient, and cost-effective alternative to traditional banking services.

However, while technological solutions offer significant benefits for the fintech sector in Côte d'Ivoire, it is essential to critically assess their implications and risks, including potential cybersecurity vulnerabilities, data privacy concerns, and regulatory compliance challenges. Fintech operators must prioritize cybersecurity as a fundamental component of their business strategy and invest in ongoing cybersecurity training, awareness programs, and incident response capabilities to mitigate cyber risks effectively. Moreover, fintech companies must ensure compliance with relevant data protection laws and regulations, such as the General Data Protection Regulation (GDPR) or the Personal Data Protection Act (PDPA), to protect the privacy and rights of individuals whose data they process.

Technological solutions and best practices are indispensable for driving innovation, efficiency, and resilience in the fintech sector in Côte d'Ivoire. By harnessing advanced technologies, adopting industry best practices, and prioritizing cybersecurity and data privacy, fintech operators can unlock new opportunities, enhance customer trust, and contribute to the growth and development of the digital economy. However, achieving these objectives requires a concerted effort from fintech companies, regulators, and other stakeholders to collaborate, innovate responsibly, and address the challenges and risks associated with technological advancements in the fintech landscape.

Conclusion

Summary of Findings

The findings of this research underscore the multifaceted nature of the fintech landscape in Côte d'Ivoire, highlighting both opportunities and challenges inherent in the rapid digitization of financial services. Across various dimensions, including regulatory frameworks, cybersecurity, consumer protection, and technological innovation, several key themes emerge, each with its implications for policymakers, regulators, industry stakeholders, and consumers.

Firstly, regulatory frameworks in Côte d'Ivoire play a crucial role in shaping the development and oversight of the fintech sector. While regulatory reforms are necessary to accommodate fintech innovation and promote market competition, there is a delicate balance to strike between fostering innovation and safeguarding financial stability and consumer protection. The Central Bank of West African States (BCEAO) and other regulatory authorities must adopt agile, risk-based approaches to regulation, ensuring that regulatory requirements are proportionate, technology-neutral, and conducive to fostering a vibrant fintech ecosystem.

Secondly, cybersecurity emerges as a critical concern in the fintech landscape, given the proliferation of cyber threats targeting financial institutions and consumers alike. Fintech operators must prioritize cybersecurity as a fundamental aspect of their business strategy, investing in robust security measures, employee training, and incident response capabilities to mitigate cyber risks effectively. Moreover, collaboration among regulators, industry stakeholders, and law enforcement agencies is essential for sharing threat intelligence, coordinating cyber defense efforts, and responding to cyber incidents in a timely and coordinated manner.

Thirdly, consumer protection remains paramount in the fintech sector, particularly as digital financial services become increasingly accessible and ubiquitous. Policymakers and regulators must implement measures to ensure that fintech services are safe, transparent, and inclusive, protecting consumers from fraud, abuse, and predatory practices. Strengthening financial literacy, promoting responsible lending practices, and establishing effective dispute resolution mechanisms are essential for building trust and confidence in fintech services among consumers.

Lastly, technological innovation holds immense potential for transforming financial services and driving economic growth in Côte d'Ivoire. Fintech operators can leverage advanced technologies such as AI, blockchain, and data analytics to enhance operational efficiency, improve customer experiences, and expand access to financial services, particularly among underserved populations. However, the adoption of technological solutions must be accompanied by robust cybersecurity measures, regulatory compliance, and ethical considerations to mitigate risks and ensure that fintech innovations benefit society as a whole.

In conclusion, the findings of this research underscore the importance of a holistic and collaborative approach to addressing the opportunities and challenges of the fintech landscape in Côte d'Ivoire. By embracing innovation, fostering regulatory certainty, prioritizing cybersecurity and consumer protection, and promoting inclusive growth, stakeholders can harness the transformative power of fintech to drive sustainable development and financial inclusion in Côte d'Ivoire and beyond.

Implications for Theory and Practice

The findings of this research carry significant implications for both theoretical frameworks and practical applications within the fintech landscape of Côte d'Ivoire. From a theoretical perspective, the evolving nature of fintech introduces new dimensions to traditional models of financial regulation, innovation theory, and consumer behavior. The emergence of fintech disrupts conventional notions of financial intermediation, challenging existing theories that may not fully capture the dynamics of digital finance and its impact on financial systems. Therefore, scholars and policymakers need to adapt theoretical frameworks to better understand the unique characteristics, drivers, and implications of fintech innovation in Côte d'Ivoire.

Moreover, the findings highlight the importance of integrating interdisciplinary perspectives, including economics, law, technology, and sociology, to develop comprehensive theories that encompass the complex interactions between regulatory environments, technological advancements, market dynamics, and consumer behaviors within the fintech ecosystem. For example, behavioral economics can provide insights into how individuals perceive and adopt fintech services, while legal and regulatory theories can inform the design of regulatory frameworks that balance innovation and consumer protection in digital finance.

From a practical standpoint, the implications of this research extend to policymakers, regulators, fintech operators, financial institutions, and consumers in Côte d'Ivoire. Firstly, policymakers and regulators must adapt existing regulatory frameworks and practices to address the unique challenges and opportunities presented by fintech innovation. This may involve revising laws, regulations, and supervisory approaches to accommodate technological advancements, promote innovation, and protect consumers while ensuring financial stability and integrity.

For example, policymakers could establish regulatory sandboxes, innovation hubs, or regulatory sandboxes to provide a controlled environment for fintech experimentation, enabling regulators to understand emerging risks and tailor regulatory responses accordingly. Additionally, regulators could collaborate with industry stakeholders, academia, and international partners to develop guidelines, standards, and best practices that promote responsible fintech innovation and compliance with regulatory requirements.

Furthermore, fintech operators and financial institutions must prioritize cybersecurity, data privacy, and regulatory compliance as fundamental aspects of their business operations. Investing in robust cybersecurity measures, employee training, and incident response capabilities is essential for mitigating cyber risks and maintaining trust and confidence in FinTech services. Moreover, fostering a culture of compliance, transparency, and ethical conduct is essential for building long-term relationships with customers and stakeholders.

Lastly, consumers play a critical role in shaping the future of fintech in Côte d'Ivoire through their adoption behaviors, preferences, and feedback. Therefore, fintech operators and financial institutions must prioritize user-centric design, accessibility, and transparency to meet the diverse needs and preferences of consumers. Educating consumers about the benefits and risks of fintech services, promoting financial literacy, and empowering them with the knowledge and tools to make informed decisions are essential for fostering trust and confidence in digital financial services.

The implications of this research for theory and practice underscore the need for a holistic and collaborative approach to address the challenges and opportunities of fintech innovation in Côte d'Ivoire. By integrating interdisciplinary perspectives, adapting regulatory frameworks, promoting cybersecurity and consumer protection, and prioritizing user-centric design, stakeholders can unlock the transformative potential of fintech to drive sustainable development and financial inclusion in Côte d'Ivoire and beyond.

Future Research Directions

The research findings provide valuable insights into the current state of the fintech landscape in Côte d'Ivoire, but they also highlight several avenues for future research that can deepen our understanding of this rapidly evolving field. These future research directions span various dimensions, including regulatory innovation, technological advancements, market dynamics, and socio-economic impacts, offering opportunities for scholars, policymakers, and industry practitioners to address emerging challenges and opportunities in the fintech sector.

One promising area for future research is the exploration of regulatory innovation and experimentation in response to fintech disruption. As fintech continues to reshape traditional financial services, policymakers and regulators must adapt regulatory frameworks to strike a balance between fostering innovation and ensuring financial stability and consumer protection. Future research could examine the effectiveness of regulatory sandboxes, innovation hubs, and other experimental approaches in facilitating fintech innovation while mitigating risks and safeguarding regulatory objectives.

Moreover, there is a need for empirical research on the adoption, usage, and impact of specific fintech innovations and business models in Côte d'Ivoire. While fintech encompasses a wide range of technologies and services, including mobile payments, digital lending, blockchain, and robo-advisory, empirical studies can provide valuable insights into the drivers and barriers to adoption, user experiences, and socio-economic impacts of these innovations on individuals, businesses, and the broader economy.

Furthermore, future research could explore the implications of technological advancements such as artificial intelligence (AI), blockchain, and big data analytics on financial inclusion, economic development, and systemic risk in Côte d'Ivoire. For example, studies could examine how AI-powered credit scoring models impact access to credit for underserved populations, or how blockchain-based solutions facilitate secure and transparent transactions in supply chain finance and remittances. By understanding the potential benefits and risks of emerging technologies, policymakers and industry stakeholders can make informed decisions to harness their transformative potential while mitigating potential drawbacks.

Additionally, there is a need for longitudinal studies that track the evolution of the fintech ecosystem over time, including changes in market structure, competitive dynamics, and regulatory landscape. Longitudinal research can provide valuable insights into trends, patterns, and trajectories of fintech development, allowing stakeholders to anticipate future developments, identify emerging risks, and adapt strategies accordingly. For example, longitudinal studies could examine how regulatory reforms impact fintech innovation and market entry over time or how changes in consumer preferences and behaviors shape the adoption and usage of fintech services.

Lastly, future research could explore the socio-economic implications of fintech innovation on financial inclusion, income inequality, and economic resilience in Côte d'Ivoire. By examining the distributional effects of fintech adoption and usage across different demographic groups, regions, and socio-economic strata, researchers can identify disparities, barriers, and opportunities for promoting inclusive fintech ecosystems that benefit all segments of society. Moreover, studies could investigate how fintech innovations contribute to job creation, entrepreneurship, and innovation ecosystems, fostering economic growth and development in Côte d'Ivoire and other emerging markets.

In conclusion, future research directions in the fintech sector of Côte d'Ivoire offer exciting opportunities to deepen our understanding of the opportunities and challenges associated with digital finance and innovation. By addressing key research gaps, leveraging interdisciplinary approaches, and collaborating across academia, industry, and government, researchers can generate valuable insights that inform evidence-based policies, strategies, and interventions to promote sustainable development, financial inclusion, and digital transformation in Côte d'Ivoire and beyond.

Fintech Adoption and Counterterrorism Measures in West Africa: A Comparative Analysis of Nigeria, Ghana, and Ivory Coast

Introduction

Overview of Fintech Adoption in West Africa

The overview of fintech adoption in West Africa paints a picture of a region experiencing significant transformation in its financial landscape. With the rapid advancement of technology and increasing connectivity, fintech has emerged as a powerful force reshaping how financial services are accessed and utilized across the continent. In countries like Nigeria, Ghana, and Ivory Coast, where traditional banking infrastructure may be limited or inaccessible to large segments of the population, fintech offers a lifeline, providing alternative means for individuals and businesses to manage their finances(Evdokimova et al., 2021).

One notable example is the rise of mobile money platforms, such as M-Pesa in Kenya and MTN Mobile Money in Ghana, which have revolutionized the way people conduct transactions, transfer money, and access financial services(Vovchenko, 2019). These platforms leverage mobile phone penetration, which is widespread across Africa, to offer inclusive and convenient banking solutions to the unbanked and underbanked populations. In Nigeria, startups like Paystack and Flutterwave have emerged as key players in facilitating online payments and e-commerce growth, demonstrating the potential of fintech to drive economic development and financial inclusion(Hendrikse et al., 2019).

However, alongside the opportunities presented by fintech, there are also challenges and barriers to adoption(Albarrak et al., 2021). Regulatory uncertainties, inadequate infrastructure, and cybersecurity concerns can hinder the growth of fintech ecosystems in West Africa. For instance, in Nigeria, where regulatory oversight of fintech activities is still evolving, startups often grapple with compliance requirements and regulatory ambiguity, which can stifle innovation and investment. Moreover, the prevalence of cyber threats, such as phishing attacks and mobile money fraud, poses risks to the security and integrity of fintech platforms, undermining trust and confidence among users(Pham et al., 2020).

Despite these challenges, the momentum behind fintech adoption in West Africa remains strong, driven by factors such as demographic shifts, urbanization, and increasing internet penetration. Governments and policymakers are recognizing the potential of fintech to drive financial inclusion and economic growth, leading to efforts to create enabling environments through regulatory reforms and supportive policies(Gontar, 2021). For instance, the Central Bank of Nigeria has introduced initiatives like the Payment Service Bank framework to encourage the participation of non-traditional players in the financial sector and promote innovation.

Fintech adoption in West Africa reveals a dynamic and evolving landscape, characterized by both opportunities and challenges. While fintech holds immense promise for expanding access to financial services and driving inclusive growth, its successful integration requires addressing regulatory, infrastructural, and security concerns(Romanov et al., 2020). By understanding the complexities of fintech adoption in the region and implementing targeted interventions, stakeholders can harness the transformative potential of technology to advance financial inclusion and strengthen economic resilience across West Africa.

Importance of Counterterrorism Measures in Fintech

The importance of counterterrorism measures in the realm of fintech cannot be overstated, especially in regions like West Africa where the threat of terrorism and financial crime looms large. Fintech platforms, with their speed, convenience, and global reach, have become attractive targets for terrorist organizations seeking to finance their operations and launder illicit funds. Therefore, safeguarding the integrity of the fintech ecosystem is not only crucial for maintaining financial stability but also for national security(Rachmawati et al., 2018).

One compelling example illustrating the nexus between fintech and terrorism is the case of Boko Haram in Nigeria. This extremist group, notorious for its violent attacks and insurgency in the northeastern region of Nigeria, has increasingly turned to digital channels to finance its operations. Reports have indicated that Boko Haram relies on various methods, including mobile money transfers and cryptocurrency transactions, to raise funds, procure weapons, and recruit new members. The anonymity and borderless nature of fintech platforms provide a cloak for terrorist actors to evade detection and exploit vulnerabilities in the financial system(Pham et al., 2020).

In response to these emerging threats, governments and regulatory authorities in West Africa have begun to recognize the urgent need for robust counterterrorism measures tailored to the fintech sector(Wonglimpiyarat, 2017). For instance, the Economic Community of West African States (ECOWAS) has established frameworks and guidelines to enhance regional cooperation and information sharing among member states in combating terrorism financing. Similarly, national governments have enacted legislation and regulatory directives to strengthen anti-money laundering (AML) and counterterrorism financing (CTF) efforts, imposing stringent requirements on fintech companies to monitor and report suspicious transactions(Still et al., 2019).

The Financial Intelligence Units (FIUs) play a crucial role in detecting and disrupting illicit financial activities in the fintech space. In Ghana, the Financial Intelligence Centre (FIC) serves as the national agency responsible for receiving, analyzing, and disseminating financial intelligence to law enforcement agencies and regulatory bodies. Through collaboration with international partners and financial institutions, FIUs can trace the flow of funds across borders, identify patterns of illicit behavior, and dismantle terrorist financing networks operating within the fintech ecosystem(Almosov, 2021).

However, the effectiveness of counterterrorism measures in fintech hinges on striking a delicate balance between security imperatives and the imperative to preserve innovation and financial inclusion (Gontar, 2021). Heavy-handed regulatory approaches that stifle fintech innovation or impose excessive compliance burdens may inadvertently drive illicit activities underground or push legitimate users towards unregulated platforms. Therefore, policymakers must adopt a risk-based approach to regulation, leveraging technology and data analytics to identify high-risk activities while facilitating legitimate financial transactions(Pantielieieva et al., 2022) .

The importance of counterterrorism measures in fintech cannot be divorced from broader national security concerns in West Africa. As fintech continues to reshape the financial landscape, policymakers, regulators, and industry stakeholders must collaborate closely to develop proactive and adaptive strategies for detecting, deterring, and disrupting terrorist financing activities(Moro-Visconti et al., 2020). By leveraging the transformative potential of fintech while mitigating associated risks, West African countries can bolster their resilience against terrorism and safeguard the integrity of their financial systems for the benefit of all stakeholders.

Objectives and Scope of the Research

The objectives and scope of research on fintech and counterterrorism in West Africa are multifaceted, aiming to address the complex interplay between financial technology and security threats in the region. At its core, the research seeks to understand how fintech adoption intersects with counterterrorism efforts, with a focus on Nigeria, Ghana, and Ivory Coast as primary case studies. The overarching objective is to provide insights that can inform policy decisions, regulatory frameworks, and industry practices to enhance the security and resilience of fintech ecosystems in West Africa.

One primary objective of the research is to assess the current state of fintech adoption in West Africa and its implications for counterterrorism measures. This involves examining the regulatory landscape, technological infrastructure, and socioeconomic factors shaping the fintech ecosystem in each country. By analyzing key indicators such as mobile penetration rates, internet connectivity, and financial inclusion metrics, the research aims to identify trends and patterns that may influence the vulnerability of fintech platforms to terrorist financing and money laundering activities.

To achieve this objective, the research will employ a combination of quantitative and qualitative methods, including data analysis and case studies. By triangulating multiple sources of information, the research aims to provide a comprehensive understanding of the dynamics driving fintech adoption and its intersection with security concerns in West Africa. Moreover, the research will adopt a comparative approach, drawing parallels and distinctions between Nigeria, Ghana, and Ivory Coast to identify best practices, common challenges, and areas for collaboration in addressing terrorist financing risks.

Another key objective of the research is to evaluate the effectiveness of existing counterterrorism measures in mitigating risks within the fintech ecosystem. This involves assessing the regulatory frameworks, institutional capacities, and enforcement mechanisms deployed by governments and regulatory authorities to combat terrorist financing and money laundering activities. By examining case studies and real-world examples of illicit transactions identified and disrupted by law enforcement agencies, the research aims to identify gaps, weaknesses, and areas for improvement in current strategies and initiatives.

Furthermore, the research seeks to explore the role of financial intelligence units (FIUs), law enforcement agencies, and international organizations in enhancing cooperation and information sharing to combat terrorist financing in the fintech sector. Drawing on lessons learned from global initiatives such as the Financial Action Task Force (FATF) and the Egmont Group, the research aims to identify opportunities for strengthening regional and international cooperation in addressing cross-border threats and illicit financial flows in West Africa.

The objectives and scope of the research encompass a holistic and multidimensional analysis of the relationship between fintech adoption and counterterrorism measures in West Africa. By examining regulatory frameworks, technological infrastructures, and enforcement mechanisms, the research aims to provide actionable insights and policy recommendations to enhance the security and resilience of fintech ecosystems in the region. Through collaboration between governments, regulatory authorities, financial institutions, and industry stakeholders, the research seeks to advance collective efforts to combat terrorist financing and safeguard the integrity of the financial system in West Africa and beyond.

Regulatory Landscape of Fintech in West Africa

Examination of Regulatory Frameworks in Nigeria, Ghana, and Ivory Coast

The examination of regulatory frameworks governing fintech in Nigeria, Ghana, and Ivory Coast reveals a complex landscape shaped by diverse socioeconomic factors, regulatory priorities, and technological capabilities(Siddiqui et al., 2022). In Nigeria, the Central Bank of Nigeria (CBN) serves as the primary regulatory authority overseeing the fintech sector, with a mandate to promote monetary stability, foster financial inclusion, and safeguard the integrity of the financial system. The CBN has implemented various initiatives and guidelines to regulate fintech activities, including the Licensing Regime for Payment Service Providers and the Guidelines for the Operations of Electronic Payment Channels. These regulatory frameworks aim to balance the need to foster innovation and competition in the fintech sector while mitigating risks related to cybersecurity, money laundering, and terrorist financing(Zarrouk et al., 2021).

In Ghana, the regulatory landscape for fintech is governed by the Bank of Ghana (BoG) and the Securities and Exchange Commission (SEC), which oversee banking and capital markets activities, respectively. The BoG has established guidelines and directives to regulate digital financial services, mobile money operations, and payment systems, with a focus on enhancing financial stability and consumer protection. Additionally, the SEC has introduced regulations to govern crowdfunding platforms, peer-to-peer lending, and other fintech-driven investment activities, aimed at promoting investor confidence and market integrity. Despite these regulatory efforts, challenges remain, including the need for greater coordination and harmonization of regulatory approaches across different sectors and agencies(Joshi et al., 2018).

In Ivory Coast, the regulatory framework for fintech is evolving rapidly in response to the growing importance of digital finance and the need to address emerging risks and opportunities(Ginsel, 2016). The Central Bank of West African States (BCEAO) plays a central role in overseeing banking and financial activities in the region, including fintech innovations. BCEAO has introduced regulations and guidelines to regulate electronic payments, mobile banking, and digital financial services, with a focus on promoting financial inclusion, enhancing consumer protection, and combating money laundering and terrorist financing. Additionally, the Ministry of Digital Economy and Postal Services has launched initiatives to promote the development of the digital economy and support fintech startups through incubation programs and funding schemes.

Despite these regulatory efforts, challenges persist in ensuring effective oversight and enforcement of fintech regulations in West Africa. Regulatory fragmentation, inconsistent enforcement, and limited technical capacity pose significant obstacles to regulatory compliance and market integrity(Mamonov, 2021). Moreover, the rapid pace of technological innovation and the borderless nature of digital finance present novel challenges for regulators and require agile and adaptive regulatory approaches. Therefore, stakeholders must collaborate closely to develop robust regulatory frameworks that strike a balance between innovation and risk management, fostering a conducive environment for fintech growth while safeguarding financial stability and security in Nigeria, Ghana, and Ivory Coast.

Comparative Analysis of Regulatory Approaches

A comparative analysis of regulatory approaches to fintech in Nigeria, Ghana, and Ivory Coast underscores both similarities and differences in how these countries approach the governance of financial technology. While each nation shares a common goal of fostering innovation and promoting financial inclusion, they exhibit distinct regulatory frameworks shaped by their unique economic, political, and institutional contexts. Nigeria, Africa's largest economy, has taken proactive steps to regulate fintech activities through the Central Bank of Nigeria (CBN), emphasizing the importance of risk management and consumer protection. The CBN's Licensing Regime for Payment Service Providers and Guidelines for the Operations of Electronic Payment Channels provide a comprehensive framework for supervising digital financial services, ensuring compliance with AML/CFT regulations, and mitigating cybersecurity risks. However, concerns have been raised about the regulatory burden placed on fintech startups and the need for greater clarity and consistency in regulatory enforcement(Jofre, 2016).

In Ghana, the regulatory landscape for fintech is characterized by a multi-agency approach, with oversight divided between the Bank of Ghana (BoG) and the Securities and Exchange Commission (SEC). The BoG regulates banking and payment systems, while the SEC oversees capital markets and investment activities. This dual regulatory structure reflects the government's commitment to maintaining financial stability and market integrity while fostering innovation in the fintech sector(Blakstad, 2018). The BoG's Digital Financial Services Guidelines and the SEC's Crowdfunding Regulations provide a framework for regulating different aspects of fintech innovation, from mobile money operations to peer-to-peer lending platforms. However, challenges remain in coordinating regulatory efforts and ensuring consistency in regulatory standards across sectors(Anderson, 2016).

In Ivory Coast, the regulatory framework for fintech is shaped by regional institutions such as the Central Bank of West African States (BCEAO) and national authorities like the Ministry of Digital Economy and Postal Services. BCEAO oversees banking and financial activities in the West African Economic and Monetary Union (WAEMU), including electronic payments and mobile banking services. The BCEAO's regulations on electronic money issuers and payment service providers aim to promote interoperability, consumer protection, and financial stability across member states. Additionally, the Ivorian government has launched initiatives to support fintech innovation and entrepreneurship, such as the National Strategy for Digital Transformation and the Fintech Innovation Fund. However, challenges persist in harmonizing regulations within the WAEMU framework and addressing cross-border issues related to fintech regulation and supervision.

This comparative analysis highlights the need for a coordinated and adaptive approach to fintech regulation in West Africa, balancing innovation and risk management to promote financial inclusion and safeguard consumer interests. By leveraging regional cooperation mechanisms and sharing best practices, Nigeria, Ghana, and Ivory Coast can strengthen their regulatory frameworks and enhance the resilience of their fintech ecosystems against emerging threats and challenges. Moreover, collaboration with international partners and engagement with industry stakeholders are essential for fostering trust and confidence in the regulatory environment and driving sustainable fintech innovation across the region.

Impact of Regulations on Fintech Innovation and Security

The impact of regulations on fintech innovation and security in Nigeria, Ghana, and Ivory Coast is a critical consideration in shaping the development and resilience of their respective financial technology ecosystems. While regulations aim to provide a framework for fostering innovation, protecting consumers, and ensuring financial stability, they can also inadvertently stifle creativity, increase compliance costs, and hinder market entry for fintech startups (Joshi et al., 2018). In Nigeria, for instance, the Central Bank's stringent requirements for obtaining licenses and compliance with AML/CFT regulations have been cited as barriers to entry for smaller fintech firms, limiting competition and innovation in the sector. Moreover, regulatory uncertainty and inconsistency in enforcement can create challenges for fintech companies seeking to navigate complex legal and compliance landscapes, potentially deterring investment and innovation(Zhang-Zhang, 2020).

Similarly, in Ghana, the multiplicity of regulatory agencies overseeing different aspects of fintech activity, including the Bank of Ghana (BoG) and the Securities and Exchange Commission (SEC), has led to overlapping mandates and regulatory gaps, posing challenges for market participants and regulators alike. While the BoG's Digital Financial Services Guidelines and the SEC's Crowdfunding Regulations aim to provide clarity and guidance for fintech firms, inconsistencies in interpretation and implementation may create confusion and compliance burdens, hindering the pace of innovation and adoption of fintech solutions. Moreover, the lack of interoperability and harmonization between different regulatory frameworks can impede the development of integrated fintech ecosystems and limit the scalability of innovative solutions (Arslanian et al., 2019).

In Ivory Coast, the regulatory environment for fintech is influenced by regional institutions such as the Central Bank of West African States (BCEAO), which oversees banking and financial activities within the West African Economic and Monetary Union (WAEMU). While BCEAO's regulations on electronic money issuers and payment service providers aim to promote interoperability and consumer protection, they may also impose rigid requirements and standards that constrain the flexibility and adaptability of fintech innovations. Furthermore, the Ivorian government's initiatives to support fintech entrepreneurship, such as the Fintech Innovation Fund, may face challenges in effectively balancing regulatory oversight with the need for promoting innovation and market competition(Ginsel, 2016).

Overall, the impact of regulations on fintech innovation and security in West Africa underscores the importance of achieving a delicate balance between regulatory objectives and industry dynamics. Regulatory frameworks should be designed to foster an enabling environment for innovation while safeguarding against risks and protecting consumer interests(Schmidt et al., 2018) . Collaboration between regulators, industry stakeholders, and policymakers is essential for ensuring that regulations are fit for purpose, responsive to market developments, and conducive to sustainable fintech growth. By adopting a forward-looking approach to regulation, West African countries can unlock the full potential of fintech innovation to drive financial inclusion, economic development, and security in the region(Blakstad et al., 2018).

Fintech Infrastructure and Adoption in Nigeria, Ghana, and Ivory Coast

Analysis of Technological Infrastructure Supporting Fintech Services

The analysis of technological infrastructure supporting fintech services in Nigeria, Ghana, and Ivory Coast reveals both opportunities and challenges in harnessing digital innovation to drive financial inclusion and economic growth. In Nigeria, where mobile phone penetration has skyrocketed in recent years, fintech startups have capitalized on the widespread adoption of smartphones and mobile internet to offer innovative solutions such as mobile banking, peer-to-peer lending, and digital payments (Jofre, 2016). Platforms like Paystack and Flutterwave have leveraged Application Programming Interfaces (APIs) and cloud-based technologies to build scalable and secure payment gateways, enabling businesses to accept online payments and streamline their financial operations. Moreover, the emergence of digital identity systems like the Bank Verification Number (BVN) has facilitated Know Your Customer (KYC) verification and enhanced the security of financial transactions, laying the groundwork for broader adoption of fintech services across the country (Sotto-Mayor, 2016).

In Ghana, the technological infrastructure supporting fintech services is characterized by a mix of mobile money platforms, payment processors, and digital banking solutions, underpinned by robust telecommunications networks and mobile banking interoperability. Mobile money operators like MTN Mobile Money and AirtelTigo Money have transformed the way people conduct transactions, transfer money, and access financial services, particularly in rural and underserved areas where traditional banking infrastructure is limited. Additionally, the interoperability of mobile money platforms with banking systems and third-party fintech apps has expanded the reach and accessibility of financial services, enabling seamless integration across different channels and enhancing the user experience for customers (Wonglimpiyarat, 2017).

In Ivory Coast, the technological infrastructure supporting fintech services is evolving rapidly, driven by investments in digital connectivity, e-government initiatives, and mobile banking innovations. The widespread adoption of mobile phones and the internet has paved the way for the growth of mobile money platforms like Orange Money and Moov Money, which offer a range of financial services including digital payments, savings, and credit. Moreover, the Ivorian government's efforts to promote digital entrepreneurship and innovation through initiatives like the National Strategy for Digital Transformation have spurred the development of fintech ecosystems and incubation hubs, fostering collaboration between startups, investors, and regulatory authorities to address common challenges and drive collective growth(Evdokimova et al., 2021).

However, despite the progress made in enhancing technological infrastructure for fintech services in West Africa, challenges remain in bridging the digital divide, ensuring cybersecurity, and addressing infrastructure gaps in rural and underserved areas. Connectivity issues, power outages, and data privacy concerns may hinder the adoption of fintech solutions among certain segments of the population, limiting their impact on financial inclusion and economic development(Moro-Visconti et al., 2020). Moreover, the rapid pace of technological innovation and the evolving nature of cyber threats require continuous investment in digital infrastructure, capacity building, and regulatory frameworks to safeguard the integrity and resilience of fintech ecosystems in

Nigeria, Ghana, and Ivory Coast. By addressing these challenges and leveraging technology to overcome barriers to financial access, West African countries can unlock the full potential of fintech to drive inclusive growth, empower communities, and enhance economic resilience in the region.

Identification of Vulnerabilities within Fintech Ecosystems

The identification of vulnerabilities within fintech ecosystems in Nigeria, Ghana, and Ivory Coast is crucial for understanding and mitigating the risks associated with digital financial services. One significant vulnerability lies in cybersecurity threats, including data breaches, phishing attacks, and malware infections, which can compromise the integrity and confidentiality of financial transactions and sensitive customer information(Pantielieieva et al., 2022) . For example, in Nigeria, the increasing reliance on digital payments and mobile banking has made consumers and businesses vulnerable to cyberattacks, with reports of fraudsters exploiting weaknesses in authentication processes and mobile banking apps to siphon funds and steal personal data. Similarly, in Ghana and Ivory Coast, the rapid adoption of mobile money platforms and digital payment solutions has attracted cybercriminals seeking to exploit vulnerabilities in software, networks, and user behavior to perpetrate fraud and financial crimes(Gontar, 2021).

Another vulnerability within fintech ecosystems is the lack of regulatory oversight and consumer protection measures, particularly in emerging markets where regulatory frameworks may be less developed or inconsistently enforced (Moro-Visconti et al., 2020). For instance, in Ghana, the proliferation of informal fintech services and unregulated lending platforms has raised concerns about predatory practices, excessive interest rates, and debt traps for vulnerable borrowers. Similarly, in Ivory Coast, the absence of comprehensive regulations governing digital financial services and electronic payments leaves consumers exposed to risks such as unauthorized transactions, unfair practices, and disputes with service providers. Moreover, the lack of transparency and accountability in fintech operations can undermine trust and confidence in the financial system, deterring individuals and businesses from fully embracing digital finance solutions (Hendrikse et al., 2019).

Furthermore, the rapid pace of technological innovation and the interconnected nature of fintech ecosystems create vulnerabilities related to system interoperability, data privacy, and third-party dependencies(Zhao et al., 2022). For example, in Nigeria, interoperability challenges between different payment systems and banks' core banking platforms can result in transaction failures, delays, and reconciliation issues, impacting user experience and financial stability. Similarly, in Ghana and Ivory Coast, concerns have been raised about the security and privacy implications of sharing personal and financial data with third-party fintech apps and service providers, raising questions about data protection laws, consent mechanisms, and user rights. Additionally, reliance on external vendors and cloud-based infrastructure exposes fintech platforms to supply chain risks, service disruptions, and vulnerabilities in software and hardware components, highlighting the importance of robust risk management practices and due diligence in vendor selection and oversight (Still et al., 2019).

The identification of vulnerabilities within fintech ecosystems in West Africa underscores the need for proactive risk management, regulatory oversight, and consumer protection measures to safeguard against emerging threats and ensure the resilience of digital financial services. By addressing cybersecurity risks, strengthening regulatory frameworks, and promoting industry collaboration and best practices, Nigeria, Ghana, and Ivory Coast can enhance the trust, security, and accessibility of fintech solutions for individuals, businesses, and governments, driving sustainable growth and inclusive development in the region.

Assessment of Fintech Adoption Rates and Trends

The assessment of fintech adoption rates and trends in Nigeria, Ghana, and Ivory Coast offers valuable insights into the evolving landscape of digital finance in West Africa. In Nigeria, the largest economy in the region, fintech adoption has experienced rapid growth driven by factors such as widespread mobile phone penetration, increasing internet connectivity, and rising demand for convenient and accessible financial services (Rachmawati et al., 2018). Platforms like Interswitch, Flutterwave, and Paystack have gained traction by offering innovative solutions for digital payments, online banking, and e-commerce, catering to the needs of consumers, businesses, and government agencies alike. Moreover, the COVID-19 pandemic has accelerated the shift towards digital payments and contactless transactions, further fueling the adoption of fintech solutions for everyday financial transactions and remote banking services (Lukianenko et al., 2021).

Similarly, in Ghana, fintech adoption rates have surged in recent years, propelled by supportive regulatory frameworks, mobile money interoperability, and government-led initiatives to promote financial inclusion and digital entrepreneurship. Mobile money platforms such as MTN Mobile Money, AirtelTigo Money, and Vodafone Cash have become ubiquitous in urban and rural areas, enabling millions of Ghanaians to access basic financial services, send and receive money, and make payments for goods and services. Additionally, the emergence of fintech startups like Zeepay, Mazzuma, and ExpressPay has diversified the fintech landscape, offering solutions for remittances, savings, lending, and insurance tailored to the needs of underserved communities and microenterprises (Romanov et al., 2020).

In Ivory Coast, fintech adoption is gaining momentum, driven by government initiatives to promote digital transformation, expand financial access, and foster innovation in the digital economy. Mobile money platforms such as Orange Money, Moov Money, and MTN Mobile Money have gained widespread acceptance, offering a range of financial services including person-to-person transfers, bill payments, and merchant transactions (Goo et al., 2020). Moreover, fintech startups like CinetPay, Finclusion, and InTouch are leveraging technology and partnerships to address specific pain points in the financial ecosystem, such as access to credit, insurance, and digital identity verification(Albarrak et al., 2021). However, challenges remain in bridging the digital divide, enhancing cybersecurity, and building trust among consumers and businesses to fully realize the potential of fintech to drive inclusive growth and economic development in the country.

Overall, the assessment of fintech adoption rates and trends in Nigeria, Ghana, and Ivory Coast reflects the transformative impact of digital finance on the way people access and manage their money in West Africa. While progress has been made in expanding access to financial services and promoting innovation in the fintech sector, challenges persist in addressing regulatory barriers, infrastructure gaps, and consumer protection concerns. By fostering collaboration between governments, regulators, industry stakeholders, and international partners, Nigeria, Ghana, and Ivory Coast can unlock the full potential of fintech to drive sustainable development, financial inclusion, and economic resilience in the region.

Socioeconomic Factors Influencing Fintech Usage

Socioeconomic factors play a crucial role in shaping the adoption and usage of fintech services in Nigeria, Ghana, and Ivory Coast, reflecting the diverse needs, preferences, and constraints of individuals and businesses across different segments of society. In Nigeria, where income inequality and financial exclusion remain significant challenges, fintech solutions have emerged as a lifeline for millions of unbanked and underbanked individuals who lack access to traditional banking services. Mobile money platforms like Paga and Quickteller have gained popularity among low-income earners, informal sector workers, and rural communities, providing a convenient and affordable means to send and receive money, pay bills, and access credit without the need for a traditional bank account(Almosov, 2021). Moreover, the youth population's increasing digital literacy and smartphone penetration have fueled the adoption of fintech solutions for online shopping, peer-to-peer lending, and investment, driving innovation and entrepreneurship in the digital economy (Pham et al., 2020).

Similarly, in Ghana, socioeconomic factors such as income levels, education, and geographic location influence fintech usage patterns and adoption rates. Mobile money adoption rates are higher in rural and underserved areas where access to traditional banking services is limited, reflecting the role of fintech in bridging the financial inclusion gap and empowering marginalized communities (Manan, 2019). Moreover, the prevalence of informal economic activities, such as small-scale farming and microenterprises, creates opportunities for fintech startups to offer tailored solutions for savings, credit, and insurance, addressing the specific needs and challenges faced by individuals and businesses operating in the informal sector. However, disparities in access to digital infrastructure, financial literacy, and trust in fintech platforms may hinder the widespread adoption of digital financial services among certain demographic groups, highlighting the importance of targeted interventions and inclusive policies to address socioeconomic barriers to fintech usage (Joshi et al., 2018).

In Ivory Coast, socioeconomic factors such as urbanization, income inequality, and employment dynamics shape the demand for fintech services and the accessibility of digital financial solutions. In urban areas like Abidjan, where the majority of the population resides, fintech adoption rates are higher due to greater access to digital infrastructure, higher levels of education, and a more diverse range of economic opportunities. Mobile money platforms like Orange Money and MTN Mobile Money have become integral to urban life, enabling residents to pay for goods and services, receive remittances, and access financial services on the go. However, in rural and remote areas where infrastructure is lacking, fintech adoption rates may be lower, posing challenges for extending financial inclusion and promoting digital entrepreneurship in underserved communities (Sotto-Mayor, 2016). Moreover, concerns about data privacy, cybersecurity, and trust in digital financial services may deter certain demographic groups, particularly older adults and low-income earners, from fully embracing fintech solutions, highlighting the need for targeted awareness campaigns and consumer protection measures to build trust and confidence in fintech platforms.

Overall, socioeconomic factors exert a profound influence on fintech usage and adoption in Nigeria, Ghana, and the Ivory Coast, shaping the demand for digital financial services, the accessibility of fintech solutions, and the regulatory environment in which fintech operates. By understanding and addressing the specific needs and constraints of different demographic groups, policymakers, regulators, and industry stakeholders can foster an inclusive and sustainable fintech ecosystem that drives economic growth, empowers individuals and businesses, and promotes financial resilience in West Africa (Schmidt et al., 2018).

Financial Crime and Terrorist Financing Risks in Fintech

Overview of Financial Crime and Terrorist Financing Methods

An overview of financial crime and terrorist financing methods provides essential context for understanding the risks and vulnerabilities within fintech ecosystems in Nigeria, Ghana, and the Ivory Coast. Financial crime encompasses a broad range of illicit activities, including money laundering, fraud, corruption, and tax evasion, which pose significant threats to the integrity and stability of the financial system (Jofre, 2016). In the context of fintech, criminals and terrorist organizations exploit technological innovations and loopholes in regulatory frameworks to launder illicit proceeds, finance illicit activities, and evade detection by law enforcement agencies. For example, in Nigeria, the prevalence of advance fee fraud schemes, also known as "419 scams," has long been a challenge for authorities, with fraudsters using email, social media, and mobile messaging platforms to deceive victims and launder money through informal channels, including mobile money agents and cryptocurrency exchanges (Zhang-Zhang, 2020).

Terrorist financing, on the other hand, involves the use of financial resources to support terrorist activities, including recruitment, training, and procurement of weapons and explosives. Terrorist organizations often rely on a variety of methods to raise funds, including extortion, kidnapping for ransom, and illicit trade in commodities such as drugs, arms, and cultural artifacts. In West Africa, groups like Boko Haram in Nigeria and Al-Qaeda in the Islamic Maghreb (AQIM) in the Sahel region have exploited porous borders, weak governance, and informal financial systems to finance their operations and expand their influence. The rise of fintech platforms and digital currencies has further complicated efforts to disrupt terrorist financing networks, as these technologies offer greater anonymity, speed, and cross-border capabilities, making it easier for terrorist actors to transfer funds and evade detection by authorities (Jutla et al., 2016).

Moreover, the convergence of financial crime and terrorist financing poses challenges for regulators, law enforcement agencies, and financial institutions tasked with detecting and preventing illicit financial activities in the fintech space (Sotto-Mayor, 2016). Traditional anti-money laundering (AML) and counterterrorism financing (CTF) measures, such as customer due diligence, transaction monitoring, and suspicious activity reporting, may be less effective in detecting illicit transactions conducted through digital channels, where anonymity and encryption technologies can obscure the identities and intentions of bad actors. For example, in Ghana, the emergence of peer-to-peer lending platforms and cryptocurrency exchanges has raised concerns about the potential for abuse by money launderers and terrorist financiers seeking to exploit regulatory gaps and vulnerabilities in the financial system (Mamonov, 2021).

Financial crime and terrorist financing methods underscore the evolving nature of threats and challenges facing fintech ecosystems in Nigeria, Ghana, and Ivory Coast. By understanding the tactics and techniques used by criminals and terrorist organizations to exploit vulnerabilities in digital financial services, policymakers, regulators, and industry stakeholders can develop proactive strategies and countermeasures to safeguard the integrity and security of the financial system. Collaboration between governments, financial institutions, and technology providers is essential for strengthening regulatory frameworks, enhancing risk management practices, and promoting greater transparency and accountability in fintech operations, ultimately mitigating the risks posed by financial crime and terrorist financing in West Africa.

Identification of Vulnerabilities within Fintech Ecosystems

The identification of vulnerabilities within fintech ecosystems is critical for understanding the potential risks and challenges that could compromise the integrity and security of digital financial services in Nigeria, Ghana, and Ivory Coast. One significant vulnerability lies in the reliance on digital infrastructure and technology, which can be prone to cyberattacks, data breaches, and system failures. Fintech platforms, including mobile banking apps, payment gateways, and cryptocurrency exchanges, are prime targets for cybercriminals seeking to exploit vulnerabilities in software, networks, and user behavior to steal funds, compromise sensitive information, and disrupt financial operations (Castro, 2019). For example, in Nigeria, the increasing adoption of mobile money and digital payments has exposed consumers and businesses to phishing scams, malware infections, and fraudulent transactions, highlighting the need for robust cybersecurity measures and user awareness campaigns to mitigate the risks of cyber threats (Arslanian et al., 2019).

Another vulnerability within fintech ecosystems is the regulatory and compliance challenges associated with emerging technologies and business models (Schmidt et al., 2018) . Fintech startups often face complex and evolving regulatory requirements, including anti-money laundering (AML), know-your-customer (KYC), and data protection regulations, which can vary across jurisdictions and pose compliance burdens for companies operating in multiple markets. In Ghana, for instance, the regulatory landscape for fintech is fragmented, with oversight divided between different agencies such as the Bank of Ghana (BoG) and the Securities and Exchange Commission (SEC), leading to inconsistencies in regulatory standards and enforcement. Moreover, the lack of regulatory clarity and guidance for innovative fintech products and services, such as decentralized finance (DeFi) platforms and non-custodial wallets, can create uncertainty for market participants and hinder the development of inclusive and responsible fintech solutions (Soon, 2021) .

Furthermore, the interconnected nature of fintech ecosystems and the reliance on third-party service providers and infrastructure create additional vulnerabilities related to supply chain risks, service disruptions, and data privacy concerns. Fintech companies often rely on cloud-based technologies, application programming interfaces (APIs), and open banking frameworks to deliver seamless and integrated financial services to customers, exposing them to dependencies on external vendors and potential points of failure. In Ivory Coast, where fintech adoption is rapidly expanding, concerns have been raised about the security and privacy implications of sharing personal and financial data with third-party fintech apps and service providers, highlighting the importance of data protection laws, consent mechanisms, and user rights. Moreover, incidents of service outages, data breaches, and unauthorized access to customer information can erode trust and confidence in FinTech platforms, undermining their viability and sustainability in the long run (Blakstad et al., 2018).

The identification of vulnerabilities within fintech ecosystems underscores the need for proactive risk management, regulatory oversight, and industry collaboration to address emerging threats and safeguard the integrity and security of digital financial services in West Africa. By strengthening cybersecurity defenses, enhancing regulatory frameworks, and promoting transparency and accountability in fintech operations, Nigeria, Ghana, and Ivory Coast can foster a resilient and inclusive fintech ecosystem that promotes financial inclusion, fosters innovation, and contributes to sustainable economic development in the region.

Case Studies and Examples of Terrorist Financing through Fintech

Examining case studies and examples of terrorist financing through fintech sheds light on the evolving tactics and strategies employed by terrorist organizations to exploit digital financial services for illicit purposes. One notable case study involves the use of cryptocurrency by terrorist groups such as ISIS and Al-Qaeda to raise funds, transfer money, and finance their operations across borders. Cryptocurrencies like Bitcoin provide anonymity, decentralization, and cross-border capabilities that make them attractive for terrorist financiers seeking to evade detection by law enforcement agencies and financial regulators (Joshi et al., 2018). For example, in 2019, the United Nations Security Council reported that ISIS was using cryptocurrency to raise funds through social media platforms, online forums, and encrypted messaging apps, enabling supporters worldwide to make anonymous donations to the group.

Another case study involves the abuse of mobile money platforms and digital payment services by terrorist organizations to launder money, disguise illicit transactions, and finance extremist activities(Siddiqui et al., 2022). In Nigeria, Boko Haram has reportedly used mobile money agents and informal hawala networks to transfer funds and pay operatives, exploiting weaknesses in regulatory oversight and compliance controls to evade detection. Moreover, the rise of peer-to-peer lending platforms and crowdfunding websites has provided new avenues for terrorist financiers to solicit donations, raise funds, and launder money through fraudulent schemes and deceptive campaigns (Zarrouk et al., 2021). For instance, in Ghana, the Financial Intelligence Centre (FIC) has issued warnings about the potential misuse of crowdfunding platforms and mobile money for terrorist financing, urging vigilance and collaboration among regulators, financial institutions, and technology providers to combat illicit financial flows and protect the integrity of the financial system.

Furthermore, the convergence of fintech and social media platforms has facilitated the dissemination of extremist propaganda, radicalization, and recruitment efforts by terrorist organizations, amplifying the impact of terrorist financing activities in cyberspace. Terrorist groups use social media platforms like Facebook, Twitter, and Telegram to solicit donations, promote fundraising campaigns, and recruit supporters, exploiting the anonymity and reach of these platforms to spread their message and solicit financial support from sympathizers worldwide (Anderson, 2016). For example, in Ivory Coast, authorities have raised concerns about the use of social media by jihadist groups to recruit and radicalize youth, highlighting the need for enhanced monitoring, counter-narrative strategies, and international cooperation to combat the online financing of terrorism and prevent violent extremism.

These case studies and examples of terrorist financing through fintech underscore the urgent need for coordinated action and collaboration among governments, regulators, financial institutions, and technology providers to detect, disrupt, and deter illicit financial activities in the digital realm. By leveraging technology, data analytics, and international cooperation mechanisms, Nigeria, Ghana, and Ivory Coast can strengthen their regulatory frameworks, enhance risk management practices, and promote greater transparency and accountability in fintech operations to mitigate the risks posed by terrorist financing and safeguard the integrity of the financial system.

Counterterrorism Measures and Strategies

Existing Counterterrorism Frameworks and Initiatives in West Africa

Existing counterterrorism frameworks and initiatives in West Africa reflect regional and international efforts to address the growing threat of terrorism and violent extremism in the region. The Economic Community of West African States (ECOWAS) and the G5 Sahel countries have established mechanisms and institutions to coordinate counterterrorism efforts, enhance intelligence sharing, and strengthen border security to prevent the spread of terrorist activities across national borders. For example, ECOWAS established the Counter-Terrorism Strategy and Implementation Plan in 2013 to promote cooperation among member states in combating terrorism, radicalization, and violent extremism, emphasizing the need for a holistic and multidimensional approach that addresses the root causes of terrorism and promotes socio-economic development, good governance, and respect for human rights.

Moreover, individual countries in West Africa have implemented national counterterrorism frameworks and legislation to combat terrorist financing, disrupt terrorist networks, and prosecute individuals involved in terrorist activities. In Nigeria, the Terrorism (Prevention) Act of 2011 criminalizes terrorist acts, provides for the freezing of terrorist assets, and establishes specialized courts and agencies to investigate and prosecute terrorism-related offenses. Similarly, in Ghana, the Anti-Money Laundering Act of 2008 and the Anti-Terrorism Act of 2008 provide legal frameworks for identifying and preventing money laundering, terrorist financing, and other financial crimes, with the Financial Intelligence Centre (FIC) serving as the national agency responsible for coordinating AML/CFT efforts and implementing international standards and best practices.

Furthermore, international organizations and donor agencies have provided technical assistance, capacity building, and financial support to strengthen the capacity of West African countries to counter terrorism and violent extremism. For example, the United Nations Office on Drugs and Crime (UNODC), in collaboration with ECOWAS and the African Union (AU), has implemented regional initiatives to enhance law enforcement cooperation, border management, and counterterrorism financing efforts in West Africa. Moreover, the Global Counterterrorism Forum (GCTF) and the Financial Action Task Force (FATF) have developed guidance and best practices to assist countries in implementing effective AML/CFT measures and combating terrorist financing through fintech and other emerging technologies.

However, despite these efforts, significant challenges remain in addressing the root causes of terrorism, strengthening institutional capacities, and promoting regional cooperation and coordination in West Africa. Weak governance, political instability, porous borders, and socioeconomic inequalities create conducive environments for terrorist groups to operate and thrive, undermining efforts to prevent and counter-terrorism in the region. Moreover, the proliferation of illicit financial activities, including money laundering, corruption, and illicit trade, poses challenges for detecting and disrupting terrorist financing networks, requiring sustained commitment and collaboration among governments, civil society, and international partners to address the multifaceted challenges posed by terrorism and violent extremism in West Africa.

Collaborative Efforts between Governments, Financial Institutions, and Fintech Companies

Collaborative efforts between governments, financial institutions, and fintech companies play a pivotal role in addressing the challenges and maximizing the opportunities presented by fintech innovation in Nigeria, Ghana, and Ivory Coast. By leveraging their respective strengths and expertise, these stakeholders can enhance regulatory compliance, promote financial inclusion, and foster innovation in the fintech ecosystem.

One significant aspect of collaboration is regulatory coordination and dialogue between governments and fintech companies (Blakstad et al., 2018). Governments have a crucial role in setting regulatory frameworks that balance innovation with consumer protection and financial stability. Fintech companies can contribute valuable insights and expertise to inform the development of regulations that are conducive to innovation while addressing the unique risks associated with digital finance (Siddiqui et al., 2022). For example, in Ghana, the Bank of Ghana (BoG) has engaged with fintech startups and industry associations to gather feedback on regulatory proposals, solicit input on emerging trends and technologies, and promote greater transparency and collaboration between regulators and industry stakeholders.

Financial institutions also play a vital role in fostering collaboration with fintech companies to expand access to financial services and drive innovation(Almosov, 2021). Traditional banks and financial service providers can partner with fintech startups to develop innovative products and solutions that address the needs of underserved and unbanked populations. For instance, in Ivory Coast, banks have partnered with mobile money operators and fintech startups to offer digital banking services, mobile payments, and microfinance solutions tailored to the needs of rural communities and informal sector workers. Moreover, financial institutions can provide fintech companies with access to infrastructure, capital, and regulatory expertise, enabling them to scale their operations and reach new markets more effectively (Pham et al., 2020).

Furthermore, collaboration between governments, financial institutions, and fintech companies is essential for strengthening cybersecurity and combating financial crime and terrorist financing in the digital era. By sharing threat intelligence, best practices, and technical resources, stakeholders can enhance the resilience of fintech ecosystems and mitigate the risks posed by cyberattacks, fraud, and illicit financial activities. For example, in Nigeria, the Central Bank has collaborated with financial institutions and technology providers to develop cybersecurity guidelines, conduct cybersecurity awareness campaigns, and establish incident response mechanisms to detect and respond to cyber threats proactively (Manan, 2019).

Overall, collaborative efforts between governments, financial institutions, and fintech companies are essential for driving sustainable growth, promoting financial inclusion, and safeguarding the integrity and security of digital financial services in Nigeria, Ghana, and Ivory Coast. By fostering partnerships, fostering innovation, and promoting responsible fintech practices, stakeholders can harness the transformative power of technology to build more resilient, inclusive, and prosperous economies in West Africa.

Evaluation of Effectiveness and Gaps in Current Strategies

The evaluation of effectiveness and gaps in current strategies for addressing fintech-related security challenges and terrorist financing in Nigeria, Ghana, and Ivory Coast reveals both successes and areas for improvement in combating financial crime and promoting security in the digital era. While significant progress has been made in enhancing regulatory frameworks, strengthening cybersecurity defenses, and promoting collaboration between governments, financial institutions, and fintech companies, persistent challenges remain in addressing the evolving nature of threats, enhancing regulatory compliance, and promoting financial inclusion (Rachmawati et al., 2018).

One area of effectiveness lies in the adoption of regulatory measures and international standards to combat money laundering and terrorist financing through fintech. Governments in West Africa have implemented AML/CFT regulations and established financial intelligence units (FIUs) to detect and prevent illicit financial activities, including those facilitated by fintech platforms. For example, Nigeria's enactment of the Terrorism (Prevention) Act and the establishment of the Nigerian Financial Intelligence Unit (NFIU) have strengthened the country's legal and institutional framework for combating terrorist financing, enhancing coordination between law enforcement agencies and financial institutions to disrupt terrorist networks and freeze terrorist assets. Similarly, in Ghana, the Anti-Money Laundering Act and the Anti-Terrorism Act provide legal frameworks for identifying and prosecuting money laundering and terrorist financing offenses, with the Financial Intelligence Centre (FIC) serving as the national agency responsible for coordinating AML/CFT efforts and implementing international standards and best practices.

However, gaps persist in the effective implementation and enforcement of AML/CFT regulations, particularly in addressing emerging risks and vulnerabilities associated with fintech innovation. Regulatory fragmentation, inconsistent enforcement, and gaps in supervisory capacity pose challenges for ensuring compliance with AML/CFT requirements and detecting suspicious transactions conducted through digital channels. Moreover, the lack of harmonization and interoperability between different regulatory frameworks and jurisdictions hinders information sharing and collaboration between countries, allowing illicit actors to exploit regulatory arbitrage and evade detection by moving funds across borders (Wonglimpiyarat, 2017). For example, in Ivory Coast, the absence of comprehensive regulations governing digital financial services and electronic payments limits the effectiveness of AML/CFT efforts and undermines efforts to combat terrorist financing and other financial crimes.

Furthermore, gaps exist in addressing the root causes of terrorism and violent extremism, including socioeconomic inequalities, political instability, and governance challenges (Lukianenko et al., 2021). While efforts to strengthen security measures and disrupt terrorist networks are essential, sustainable solutions require addressing the underlying drivers of radicalization and extremism through inclusive development, good governance, and community engagement. For example, initiatives that promote youth empowerment, education, and economic opportunities can help address the grievances and vulnerabilities that terrorists exploit to recruit and radicalize individuals, reducing the appeal of extremist ideologies and strengthening resilience against terrorism in the long term.

While current strategies have made progress in addressing fintech-related security challenges and terrorist financing in West Africa, gaps remain in regulatory compliance, international cooperation, and addressing the root causes of terrorism. By strengthening regulatory frameworks, enhancing supervisory capacity, and promoting socioeconomic development and community resilience, Nigeria, Ghana, and Ivory Coast can build more resilient and inclusive financial ecosystems that foster innovation, promote stability, and mitigate the risks posed by financial crime and terrorism in the digital age.

Recommendations and Future Directions

Policy Recommendations for Strengthening Fintech Security and Counterterrorism Efforts

Policy recommendations for strengthening fintech security and counterterrorism efforts in Nigeria, Ghana, and Ivory Coast are crucial for mitigating risks, enhancing resilience, and promoting trust in digital financial services. Firstly, governments should prioritize the development and implementation of comprehensive regulatory frameworks that address the unique challenges posed by fintech innovation while ensuring compliance with international standards and best practices. For example, regulators can establish clear guidelines and requirements for fintech companies to enhance cybersecurity, customer due diligence, and transaction monitoring, fostering a culture of compliance and accountability in the fintech ecosystem.

Secondly, governments should invest in capacity building and training programs to enhance the skills and expertise of regulators, law enforcement agencies, and financial institutions in detecting, investigating, and prosecuting financial crimes and terrorist financing activities facilitated by fintech. By providing specialized training on emerging technologies, threat intelligence analysis, and investigative techniques, authorities can strengthen their capabilities to identify and disrupt illicit financial flows, enhance collaboration with industry stakeholders, and promote a coordinated response to fintech-related security challenges.

Moreover, governments should prioritize international cooperation and information-sharing mechanisms to address cross-border threats and vulnerabilities in the digital financial ecosystem. By strengthening partnerships with regional and international organizations, such as ECOWAS, the AU, and the United Nations, governments can enhance information exchange, harmonize regulatory approaches, and coordinate joint initiatives to combat terrorist financing and promote cybersecurity in West Africa. For example, the establishment of regional AML/CFT task forces and joint investigation teams can facilitate cooperation between countries in investigating and prosecuting transnational financial crimes and terrorist activities.

Additionally, governments should promote public-private partnerships and industry collaboration to enhance cybersecurity resilience, promote responsible innovation, and protect consumers from fraud and financial scams. Fintech companies, financial institutions, and technology providers can work together to develop and implement industry standards, best practices, and technological solutions to address cybersecurity threats, safeguard customer data, and strengthen the integrity of digital financial services. For instance, initiatives such as the Financial Services Information Sharing and Analysis Center (FS-ISAC) and the Cyber Threat Intelligence Sharing Platform (CTISP) facilitate collaboration between industry participants to share threat intelligence, coordinate incident response, and strengthen cyber defenses against common adversaries.

Furthermore, governments should prioritize efforts to address the root causes of terrorism and violent extremism through inclusive development, social cohesion, and community engagement initiatives. By investing in education, youth empowerment, and economic opportunities, governments can mitigate the drivers of radicalization and extremism, build resilient communities, and reduce the appeal of terrorist ideologies. For example, programs that promote entrepreneurship, vocational training, and job creation can provide alternatives to radicalization and empower individuals to resist extremist influences, fostering a culture of tolerance, resilience, and peace in West Africa.

In conclusion, policy recommendations for strengthening fintech security and counterterrorism efforts in Nigeria, Ghana, and Ivory Coast should focus on enhancing regulatory frameworks, capacity building, international cooperation, public-private partnerships, and community resilience initiatives. By implementing these recommendations, governments can foster a secure and inclusive fintech ecosystem that promotes innovation, financial inclusion, and sustainable development while mitigating the risks posed by financial crime and terrorism in the digital age.

Areas for Further Research and Development

Areas for further research and development in the realm of fintech security and counterterrorism efforts in West Africa present ample opportunities to deepen our understanding, enhance strategies, and foster innovation in addressing emerging threats and challenges. One promising area for research is the study of emerging technologies and their implications for fintech security and counterterrorism. Technologies such as blockchain, artificial intelligence (AI), and biometrics hold the potential to revolutionize financial services by enhancing security, improving efficiency, and reducing costs. However, their adoption also raises new challenges and risks, including cybersecurity vulnerabilities, data privacy concerns, and regulatory compliance issues. Research in this area can explore the potential benefits and risks of these technologies, develop best practices for their responsible use, and identify strategies to mitigate associated risks and vulnerabilities.

Another area for research is the analysis of the impact of regulatory frameworks on fintech innovation and security in West Africa. While regulations are essential for promoting consumer protection, financial stability, and integrity in the financial system, overly burdensome or outdated regulations can stifle innovation, hinder competition, and impede the adoption of fintech solutions. Research can assess the effectiveness of existing regulatory frameworks in balancing innovation with security and compliance, identify gaps and inconsistencies in regulatory approaches, and propose regulatory reforms and policy interventions to foster a conducive environment for fintech development while safeguarding against financial crime and terrorist financing.

Furthermore, research into the socioeconomic factors influencing fintech adoption and usage patterns in West Africa can provide valuable insights into the drivers and barriers to financial inclusion, digital literacy, and trust in fintech platforms. By understanding the needs, preferences, and behaviors of diverse demographic groups, policymakers, regulators, and industry stakeholders can design targeted interventions and tailored solutions to promote greater uptake of fintech services, reduce inequalities, and empower underserved communities. For example, research could explore the impact of gender, age, income, and education levels on fintech adoption and usage, identify strategies to address accessibility barriers and enhance user experience, and promote financial education and literacy programs to empower consumers to make informed decisions about their financial well-being.

Moreover, research into the effectiveness of public-private partnerships and industry collaboration in combating financial crime and terrorist financing through fintech can provide valuable insights into best practices, challenges, and opportunities for cooperation. By evaluating existing initiatives, case studies, and collaborative frameworks, researchers can identify key success factors, lessons learned, and areas for improvement in enhancing cybersecurity resilience, promoting regulatory compliance, and fostering trust and transparency in the fintech ecosystem. For example, the research could assess the impact of information-sharing platforms, joint exercises, and public-private dialogue mechanisms in strengthening the resilience of critical infrastructure, enhancing threat intelligence sharing, and promoting a coordinated response to cyber threats and terrorist financing activities.

Areas for further research and development in fintech security and counterterrorism efforts in West Africa encompass a wide range of topics, including emerging technologies, regulatory frameworks, socioeconomic factors, and public-private partnerships. By advancing knowledge, promoting collaboration, and fostering innovation in these areas, researchers, policymakers, and industry stakeholders can contribute to building a more secure, inclusive, and resilient fintech ecosystem that promotes financial stability, fosters innovation, and safeguards against financial crime and terrorist threats in the digital age.

Conclusion: Implications for Fintech Industry and National Security in West Africa

In conclusion, the implications for the fintech industry and national security in West Africa are multifaceted and underscore the need for concerted efforts to balance innovation, security, and resilience in the digital financial ecosystem. The rapid growth of fintech in Nigeria, Ghana, and Ivory Coast has brought about transformative changes, offering unprecedented opportunities for financial inclusion, economic growth, and technological innovation. However, alongside these opportunities come significant challenges, including cybersecurity threats, regulatory complexities, and the risk of terrorist financing, which have implications for both the fintech industry and national security.

For the fintech industry, the evolving threat landscape highlights the importance of investing in robust cybersecurity measures, regulatory compliance, and risk management practices to safeguard against emerging risks and vulnerabilities. Fintech companies must prioritize security by design, embedding cybersecurity principles into the development and deployment of their products and services. By adopting a proactive approach to cybersecurity, fintech companies can build trust and confidence among consumers, investors, and regulators, enhancing their resilience and competitiveness in the market.

Moreover, the fintech industry must actively collaborate with governments, financial institutions, and technology partners to strengthen regulatory compliance, enhance information sharing, and promote industry standards and best practices. By fostering public-private partnerships and industry collaboration, fintech companies can contribute to a more secure, transparent, and resilient financial ecosystem that promotes financial stability and integrity in West Africa.

For national security, the rise of fintech presents both opportunities and challenges in addressing the evolving threat landscape posed by financial crime and terrorist financing. Governments must adopt a holistic and multidimensional approach to national security that encompasses regulatory reform, law enforcement coordination, and community engagement initiatives to address the root causes of terrorism and violent extremism. By investing in education, social cohesion, and economic development, governments can mitigate the drivers of radicalization and extremism, foster resilience, and build stronger, more cohesive societies that are less susceptible to terrorist ideologies.

Furthermore, governments must enhance regulatory frameworks and law enforcement capabilities to detect, disrupt, and deter illicit financial activities facilitated by fintech platforms. By strengthening AML/CFT regulations, enhancing supervisory capacity, and promoting international cooperation, governments can enhance their ability to combat money laundering, terrorist financing, and other financial crimes in the digital age.

The implications for the fintech industry and national security in West Africa underscore the importance of collaboration, innovation, and resilience in addressing emerging threats and challenges. By working together, governments, financial institutions, fintech companies, and other stakeholders can build a more secure, inclusive, and sustainable financial ecosystem that promotes economic prosperity, fosters innovation, and safeguards against financial crime and terrorist threats in the digital age.

References

Albarrak, Mansour S., and Sara A. A. "FinTech: Ecosystem, Opportunities and Challenges in Saudi Arabia." Journal of Risk and Financial Management 14, no. 10 (September 29, 2021): 460. http://dx.doi.org/10.3390/jrfm14100460.

Almosov, Aleksandr, Svetlana B., Oksana D., Sofya P., and Elena T. "Peculiarities of development of the digital financial ecosystem." SHS Web of Conferences 109 (2021): 01004. http://dx.doi.org/10.1051/shsconf/202110901004.

Anderson, N. "Corporate Venture Capital - The New Power Broker in the FinTech Innovation Ecosystem." In The FinTech Book, 186–89. Chichester, UK: John Wiley & Sons, Ltd, 2016. http://dx.doi.org/10.1002/9781119218906.ch49.

Arslanian, Henri, and Fabrice F. "Fintech and the Future of the Financial Ecosystem." In The Future of Finance, 201–16. Cham: Springer International Publishing, 2019. http://dx.doi.org/10.1007/978-3-030-14533-0_16.

Blakstad, Sofie. FinTech revolution: Universal inclusion in the new financial ecosystem. 2018.

Blakstad, Sofie, and Robert A. "Ecosystem vs Ecosystem and Revolution vs Evolution." In FinTech Revolution, 3–17. Cham: Springer International Publishing, 2018. http://dx.doi.org/10.1007/978-3-319-76014-8_1.

Bernards, N. Poverty finance and the durable contradictions of colonial capitalism: placing 'financial inclusion' in the long run in Ghana. Geoforum; Journal of Physical, Human, and Regional Geosciences, 123, 89–98. 2021

Castro, Paola Corrêa D'Albuquerque e. "Understanding FinTech ecosystem evolution through service innovation and socio-technical system perspective." Master's thesis, 2019. https://hdl.handle.net/10216/124053.

Chironga, M., De Grandis, H., and Zouaoui, Y. Mobile financial services in Africa: Winning the battle for the consumer, McKinsey & Company, September 1. 2017. Available at: https://www.mckinsey.com/industries/financial-services/our-insights/mobile-financial-services-in-africa-winning-the-battle-for-the-customer.

Deloitte. Leveraging digital to unlock the base of the pyramid market in Africa: waves of digital innovation in financial services. 2017. Available at https://www2.deloitte.com/content/dam/Deloitte/za/Documents/africa/za_Digital_BoP.pdf

Evdokimova, Yuliya V., and Olga V. S. "World fintech: main trends." Mezhdunarodnaja jekonomika (The World Economics), no. 1 (January 1, 2021): 14–26. http://dx.doi.org/10.33920/vne-04-2101-02.

Ginsel, D. "The Journey Towards an Integrated FinTech Ecosystem - The Netherlands." In The FinTech Book, 48–50. Chichester, UK: John Wiley & Sons, Ltd, 2016. http://dx.doi.org/10.1002/9781119218906.ch12.

Gontar, L. O. "Smart approaches in the digital financial ecosystem: fintech in the context of the use of digital platforms and smart control." E-Management 4, no. 2 (July 31, 2021): 44–50. http://dx.doi.org/10.26425/2658-3445-2021-4-2-44-50.

Goo, Jayoung J., and Joo-Yeun H. "The Impact of the Regulatory Sandbox on the Fintech Industry, with a Discussion on the Relation between Regulatory Sandboxes and Open Innovation." Journal of Open Innovation: Technology, Market, and Complexity 6, no. 2 (June 18, 2020): 43. http://dx.doi.org/10.3390/joitmc6020043.

Guermond, V. Contesting new 'development frontiers': The uneven financial incorporation of remittance flows and households in Senegal and Ghana. Thesis (PhD). Queen Mary University of London. 2019.

Hendrikse, Reijer, Michiel van Meeteren, and David B. "Strategic coupling between finance, technology, and the state: Cultivating a Fintech ecosystem for incumbent finance." Environment and Planning A: Economy and Space 52, no. 8 (November 11, 2019): 1516–38. http://dx.doi.org/10.1177/0308518x19887967.

Jofre, Oscar A. "Regulated Crowdfunding Ecosystems." In The FinTech Book, 117–19. Chichester, UK: John Wiley & Sons, Ltd, 2016. http://dx.doi.org/10.1002/9781119218906.ch30.

Joshi, Mahesh K., and J. R. Klein. Technological Disruption in Global Finance. Oxford University Press, 2018. http://dx.doi.org/10.1093/oso/9780198827481.003.0004.

Jutla, Sukhi, and Narendiran Sundararajan. "India's FinTech Ecosystem." In The FinTech Book, 56–57. Chichester, UK: John Wiley & Sons, Ltd, 2016. http://dx.doi.org/10.1002/9781119218906.ch15.

Kvangraven, I.H., Koddenbrock, K., and Sylla, N.S. Financial subordination and uneven financialization in 21st century Africa. Community Development Journal, 56 (1), 119–140. 2021.

KPMG. FinTech in Nigeria: Understanding the value proposition, November. 2016/ Available at: https://assets.kpmg/content/dam/kpmg/ng/pdf/ng-fintech-in-nigeria-understanding-the-value-proposition.pdf.

Lukianenko, Iryna, and Yevhen R. "Global Investment and Development Trends in the Fintech Secto." Scientific Papers NaUKMA. Economics 6, no. 1 (July 30, 2021): 90–98. http://dx.doi.org/10.18523/2519-4739.2021.6.1.90-98.

Mbiti, I., and Weil, D. N. Mobile banking: the impact of M-Pesa in Kenya, National Bureau of Economic Research, Working Paper 1712. 2011. Available at http://www.nber.org/papers/w17129

Mamonov, Stanislav. "The Role of Information Technology in Fintech Innovation: Insights from the European Fintech Ecosystem." In Hawaii International Conference on System Sciences. Hawaii International Conference on System Sciences, 2021. http://dx.doi.org/10.24251/hicss.2021.612.

Manan, Yulianti. "Sistem Integrasi Proteksi & Manajemen Resiko Platform Fintech peer to peer (P2P) Lending dan Payment Gateway untuk Meningkatkan Akslerasi Pertumbuhan UMKM 3.0." Ihtifaz: Journal of Islamic Economics, Finance, and Banking 2, no. 1 (June 24, 2019): 73. http://dx.doi.org/10.12928/ijiefb.v2i1.847.

Moro-Visconti, Roberto, Maria C. Q., and Mariarosa B. "Matching financial closeness with social distancing: Networking digital platforms within a corporate governance ecosystem." Corporate Ownership and Control 18, no. 1 (2020): 96–109. http://dx.doi.org/10.22495/cocv18i1art8.

Nguena, C. L. Mobile banking and financial services development in Africa. Working Paper Series N° 323. Abidjan, Côte d'Ivoire: African Development Bank. 2019.

Pantielieieva, Nataliia, Kseniia P., Natalia T., Yuliia Z., Svitlana Z., and Nataliya R. "Current stage of formation of the financial intermediation ecosystem in the context of digitalization." Ekonomski pregled 73, no. 2 (2022): 215–39. http://dx.doi.org/10.32910/ep.73.2.3.

Pham, Huong T., and Tuan A. D. "Impacts of Fintech to Finance-Banking activities and recommendation for Finance-Banking industry in Vietnam." Journal of Mining and Earth Sciences 61, no. 5 (October 31, 2020): 104–10. http://dx.doi.org/10.46326/jmes.ktqtkd2020.14.

Rachmawati, Ivany, Marcella W., Adityo N., and Peri A. Manaf. "Role of Fintech Services Providers and Stakeholders as Drivers in Digital Payment Ecosystems." In 4th Sriwijaya Economics, Accounting, and Business Conference. SCITEPRESS - Science and Technology Publications, 2018. http://dx.doi.org/10.5220/0008441404680475.

Romanov, Vadim A., and Veronika V. Khubulova. "The fintech industry: key technologies and directions of development of the financial digitization." RUDN Journal of Economics 28, no. 4 (December 15, 2020): 700–712. http://dx.doi.org/10.22363/2313-2329-2020-28-4-700-712.

Schmidt, Julian, Paul D., and Ingrid S. "Charting the Emerging Financial Services Ecosystem of Fintechs and Banks: Six Types of Data-Driven Business Models in the Fintech Sector." In Hawaii International Conference on System Sciences. Hawaii International Conference on System Sciences, 2018. http://dx.doi.org/10.24251/hicss.2018.625.

Siddiqui, Zakia, and Claudio A. R. "FinTech and FinTech ecosystem: A review of literature." Risk Governance and Control: Financial Markets and Institutions 12, no. 1 (2022): 63–73. http://dx.doi.org/10.22495/rgcv12i1p5.

Soon, Sonia. "Improving the digital financial services ecosystem through collaboration of regulators and FinTech companies." In FinTech, Artificial Intelligence and the Law, 46–63. London: Routledge, 2021. http://dx.doi.org/10.4324/9781003020998-6.

Sotto-Mayor, Sofia F. "Millennium BCP′s strategic positioning in the FinTech ecosystem." Master's thesis, 2016. http://hdl.handle.net/10362/20559.

Still, Kaisa, Ilkka L., and Marko S. "Innovation Relationships in the Emergence of Fintech Ecosystems." In Hawaii International Conference on System Sciences. Hawaii International Conference on System Sciences, 2019. http://dx.doi.org/10.24251/hicss.2019.765.

Oppong, K. and Mattern, M. African digital credit go West, CGAP blog, January 6. 2020. Available at: https://www.cgap.org/blog/african-digital-credit-goes-west.

Vovchenko, N. G., S. S. Galazova, A. A. Sopchenko, and O. S. Dzhu. "FinTech Ecosystem as an Instrument of Sustainable Development Provision." International Journal of Economics and Business Administration VII, Special Issue 2 (January 1, 2019): 147–55. http://dx.doi.org/10.35808/ijeba/379.

Zarrouk, Hajer, Teheni El Ghak, and Abderazak B. "Exploring Economic and Technological Determinants of FinTech Startups' Success and Growth in the United Arab Emirates." Journal of Open Innovation: Technology, Market, and Complexity 7, no. 1 (February 1, 2021): 50. http://dx.doi.org/10.3390/joitmc7010050.

Zhang-Zhang, Yingying, Sylvia R., and Jay R. "An Eco-Systematic View of Cross-Sector Fintech: The Case of Alibaba and Tencent." Sustainability 12, no. 21 (October 27, 2020): 8907. http://dx.doi.org/10.3390/su12218907.

Zhao, Jinsong, Xinghao L., Chin-Hsien Yu, Shi C., and Chi-Chuan Lee. "Riding the FinTech innovation wave: FinTech, patents, and bank performance." Journal of International Money and Finance 122 (April 2022): 102552. http://dx.doi.org/10.1016/j.jimonfin.2021.102552.

Wonglimpiyarat, J. "FinTech banking industry: a systemic approach." foresight 19, no. 6 (November 13, 2017): 590–603. http://dx.doi.org/10.1108/fs-07-2017-0026.

Fintech Integration within the African Union Peace and Security Architecture: Regulations, Practices, and Implications

Introduction

Context and Objectives

The context of this research lies at the intersection of two rapidly evolving domains: financial technology (fintech) and peace and security within the African Union (AU). Fintech has emerged as a disruptive force in the financial industry, offering innovative solutions that have the potential to transform the way individuals and businesses access and manage financial services. In the African context, where traditional banking infrastructure is often lacking, fintech presents an opportunity to leapfrog traditional barriers to financial inclusion and stimulate economic growth. However, alongside these opportunities come significant security challenges, ranging from cybersecurity threats to concerns about illicit financial activities.

The primary objective of this research is to critically analyze the integration of fintech within the AU Peace and Security Architecture, with a focus on regulations, practices, and implications. By examining the regulatory frameworks governing fintech within the AU context, this study seeks to understand the extent to which existing policies address security concerns while fostering innovation. Moreover, through case studies of fintech implementation in AU member states, the research aims to identify socio-economic factors influencing adoption and assess the effectiveness of current practices in mitigating security risks.

For example, in examining fintech regulation within the AU, the research may analyze the recently introduced Payment Systems Act in Ghana, which aims to regulate electronic payments and promote financial inclusion while addressing cybersecurity risks and protecting consumer rights. By critically assessing the strengths and weaknesses of such regulatory frameworks, the study can offer recommendations for enhancing regulatory coherence and effectiveness across AU member states.

Similarly, in exploring the implementation of fintech solutions, the research may examine the success story of Kenya's M-Pesa mobile money platform, which has revolutionized financial services in the country and become a model for fintech innovation globally. By analyzing the socio-economic factors that contributed to M-Pesa's success, such as widespread mobile phone penetration and a supportive regulatory environment, the study can identify key drivers of fintech adoption and inform strategies for promoting inclusive and secure fintech ecosystems elsewhere in Africa.

Overall, the context and objectives of this research underscore the importance of addressing the dual imperatives of fostering fintech innovation and safeguarding against security risks within the AU context. By critically analyzing regulations, practices, and implications, the study aims to generate actionable insights that can inform policy decisions, enhance regulatory coherence, and promote sustainable fintech development across the continent.

Methodology

In conducting qualitative analysis for this research, a multifaceted approach will be employed to comprehensively examine the regulatory frameworks, implementation practices, and security implications of fintech within the African Union (AU) context. Qualitative analysis allows for in-depth exploration of complex phenomena, providing nuanced insights into the dynamics shaping fintech integration and its impact on peace and security.

One key aspect of the qualitative methodology involves the examination of regulatory documents, policy papers, and official publications issued by the AU and its member states. These documents offer valuable insights into the evolving landscape of fintech regulation, highlighting key policy priorities, regulatory frameworks, and strategic objectives. For example, the AU's Digital Financial Services Policy Framework and Implementation Guidelines provide a comprehensive overview of the organization's approach to promoting inclusive and secure fintech ecosystems across Africa. By critically analyzing these documents, the research can assess the coherence, effectiveness, and alignment of fintech regulations with broader peace and security objectives. Case studies of fintech implementation in select AU member states will also be conducted to enrich the qualitative analysis. These case studies offer contextualized insights into the socio-economic factors influencing fintech adoption, the regulatory approaches adopted by different countries, and the security implications of fintech integration. For example, a case study of Nigeria's regulatory sandbox initiative, which provides a controlled environment for testing innovative fintech solutions, can illuminate the practical challenges and opportunities associated with regulatory experimentation. Similarly, a case study of South Africa's efforts to combat cybercrime in the fintech sector can offer insights into the effectiveness of regulatory measures in mitigating security risks.

Qualitative analysis serves as a robust methodological approach for uncovering the complexities, nuances, and contextual variations inherent in fintech integration within the AU Peace and Security Architecture. Through insights from regulatory documents and case studies, the research aims to generate a holistic understanding of the regulatory, practical, and security dimensions of fintech within the AU context. Through critical analysis and interpretation of qualitative data, the study seeks to identify actionable recommendations for policymakers, regulators, and other stakeholders to promote inclusive, resilient, and secure fintech ecosystems across Africa.

Fintech Regulation in the AU

Overview of Regulatory Frameworks

Within the African Union (AU), the regulatory frameworks concerning fintech intersect with various sectors, including finance, telecommunications, and data protection, while also considering broader peace and security concerns. One prominent regulatory framework relevant to fintech within the AU context is the AU Digital Financial Services Policy Framework and Implementation Guidelines. This framework, developed by the AU's Department of Economic Affairs, provides overarching principles and strategies for promoting digital financial inclusion and innovation while ensuring consumer protection and financial stability (Gumedze, 2011). It emphasizes the importance of regulatory harmonization, interoperability, and collaboration among AU member states to create an enabling environment for fintech development across Africa.

In addition to continental-level initiatives, several AU member states have introduced their regulatory frameworks specific to fintech. For example, in Kenya, the Central Bank has established regulatory sandboxes to facilitate the testing of innovative fintech solutions in a controlled environment (Tchamyou, 2019). This approach allows fintech firms to experiment with new products and services while regulators monitor their impact and assess potential risks.

Similarly, Nigeria's Central Bank has implemented guidelines for the regulation of payment service providers and mobile money operators, outlining licensing requirements, operational standards, and cybersecurity protocols to ensure the integrity and stability of the financial system (Philippon, 2016).

Moreover, the regulatory frameworks for fintech within the AU context are closely intertwined with broader peace and security considerations, particularly in addressing cybersecurity threats and mitigating risks associated with illicit financial activities (Solf, 2014). The AU's Peace and Security Architecture, comprising institutions such as the African Peace and Security Council (APSC) and the African Standby Force (ASF), plays a crucial role in addressing emerging security challenges, including those arising from fintech (Stewart et al., 2018). The AU has recognized the need for enhanced collaboration between its peace and security institutions and relevant stakeholders in the fintech ecosystem. For example, the AU's Peace and Security Council (PSC) regularly convenes meetings and consultations with representatives from the financial sector, technology companies, and regulatory bodies to discuss emerging security threats and explore opportunities for cooperation. These engagements provide a platform for sharing expertise, exchanging information, and developing joint strategies to address fintech-related security risks effectively(Glas, 2018). While the primary focus of these institutions is on traditional security threats such as conflict and terrorism, there is increasing recognition of the need to address non-traditional security risks, including cyber threats and financial crimes facilitated by fintech.

To this end, the AU has taken steps to integrate fintech considerations into its peace and security strategies (Joshua et al., 2017). For example, the AU's Cyber Security Convention (AUCC) aims to promote cooperation among member states in combating cyber threats and enhancing cybersecurity resilience. While the primary focus of the convention is on cybersecurity in the context of information and communication technologies (ICT), it also encompasses fintech-related cyber risks. The AUCC encourages member states to develop comprehensive national cybersecurity strategies that address emerging threats, including those arising from the proliferation of fintech platforms and services. By promoting collaboration and information sharing, the AUCC seeks to strengthen the AU's collective response to cyber threats and safeguard the integrity of digital financial systems (Munlo et al.,2013). Additionally, the AU's Financial Action Task Force (FATF) regional bodies, such as the Eastern and Southern Africa Anti-Money Laundering Group (ESAAMLG) and the Inter-Governmental Action Group against Money Laundering in West Africa (GIABA), provide platforms for coordinating efforts to combat money laundering and terrorist financing facilitated by fintech (Nanziri,2017).

In addition to these institutional efforts, the AU has emphasized the importance of capacity building and awareness raising in integrating fintech considerations into its peace and security strategies (Gardachew,2020). The AU's African Centre for the Study and Research on Terrorism (ACSRT), for instance, offers training programs and workshops on cybersecurity and financial crime prevention for law enforcement agencies and other relevant stakeholders across Africa. These capacity-building initiatives aim to enhance the AU member states' ability to identify, investigate, and mitigate fintech-related security risks, thereby strengthening the AU's collective resilience to emerging threats (Engel, 2014).

Despite these efforts, challenges remain in effectively integrating fintech into the AU Peace and Security Architecture. Regulatory fragmentation, inadequate capacity, and limited resources constrain the AU's ability to address emerging security risks associated with fintech effectively. Moreover, the rapid pace of technological innovation and the borderless nature of fintech transactions present ongoing challenges for regulators and policymakers seeking to stay ahead of evolving threats.

Analysis of Regulations

The analysis of regulations concerning fintech within the African Union (AU) context requires a critical examination of the regulatory frameworks governing financial technology across AU member states and their alignment with broader peace and security objectives. One key aspect of this analysis involves assessing the coherence and effectiveness of existing regulations in addressing security risks associated with fintech while fostering innovation and financial inclusion (Abrahamyan, 2019).

For example, the regulatory landscape in Kenya offers insights into the complexities of balancing regulatory oversight with fostering fintech innovation. The Central Bank of Kenya has implemented regulatory sandboxes to provide a controlled environment for fintech firms to test innovative products and services (Kang, 2016). While these sandboxes promote experimentation and innovation, their effectiveness in mitigating security risks such as cybersecurity threats and financial crimes requires scrutiny (Ouma, 2017).

Similarly, in Nigeria, the Central Bank has introduced guidelines for the regulation of payment service providers and mobile money operators to promote financial inclusion and consumer protection (Nanziri,2017). However, challenges persist in effectively enforcing these regulations and addressing emerging security threats such as cyberattacks and money laundering facilitated by fintech platforms. The effectiveness of regulations in mitigating these risks depends on factors such as enforcement capacity, regulatory oversight, and collaboration among stakeholders (Fuster,2019).

At the continental level, the AU's Digital Financial Services Policy Framework and Implementation Guidelines provide overarching principles and strategies for promoting fintech innovation while ensuring consumer protection and financial stability. While this framework offers a comprehensive roadmap for addressing regulatory challenges and fostering an enabling environment for fintech development, its effectiveness depends on the willingness and capacity of AU member states to implement and enforce its provisions. Moreover, the framework's integration with broader peace and security strategies requires ongoing coordination and collaboration among AU institutions and relevant stakeholders (Badejo,2008).

Furthermore, the analysis of regulations within the context of the AU Peace and Security Architecture involves examining the role of peace and security institutions in addressing fintech-related security risks. While the primary focus of institutions such as the African Peace and Security Council (APSC) and the African Standby Force (ASF) is on traditional security threats, there is a growing recognition of the need to address non-traditional security risks, including cyber threats and financial crimes facilitated by fintech. Integrating fintech considerations into peace and security strategies requires enhanced collaboration and information sharing among AU institutions, regulatory bodies, and relevant stakeholders(Hammed, 2015).

Challenges in Regulation

Regulating fintech within the African Union (AU) presents a myriad of challenges, particularly within the context of the AU Peace and Security Architecture(Wood,2012). One significant challenge is the regulatory fragmentation across AU member states, which creates inconsistencies in licensing requirements, compliance standards, and oversight mechanisms. Each country adopts its approach to regulating fintech, leading to a lack of harmonization and coordination at the continental level. For instance, while some countries may have robust regulatory frameworks in place to address cybersecurity threats and financial crimes facilitated by fintech, others may have limited capacity or resources to enforce regulations effectively. This fragmentation hinders the AU's ability to develop cohesive regulatory strategies and undermines efforts to combat emerging security risks collectively(Munlo et al.,2013).

Moreover, the rapid pace of technological innovation often outpaces the ability of regulators to adapt and respond effectively. Regulators face challenges in keeping pace with emerging fintech solutions, such as decentralized finance (DeFi), blockchain-based financial services, and artificial intelligence (AI)-powered robo-advisors (Bianchetti, 2018). For example, the rise of cryptocurrencies and blockchain technology presents novel regulatory challenges related to investor protection, market integrity, and financial stability. Regulators must grapple with complex legal and technical issues in formulating appropriate regulatory responses, which may lag behind technological developments.

Furthermore, the cross-border nature of fintech transactions complicates regulatory oversight and enforcement efforts within the AU context(Solf, 2014). Fintech platforms operate across multiple jurisdictions, making it challenging for regulators to assert jurisdiction and enforce compliance with local regulations. For example, peer-to-peer lending platforms and digital asset exchanges may facilitate transactions involving users from different countries, raising questions about regulatory jurisdiction, cross-border data flows, and international cooperation. The lack of standardized regulatory frameworks for cross-border fintech transactions exacerbates regulatory uncertainty and creates opportunities for regulatory arbitrage and jurisdictional conflicts (Demirgüç-Kunt, 2018).

Additionally, the emergence of non-traditional actors in the fintech space, such as technology companies, startups, and decentralized autonomous organizations (DAOs), presents challenges for traditional regulatory frameworks within the AU context(Gumedze, 2011). Unlike traditional financial institutions, these actors may operate outside the purview of existing regulatory regimes, blurring the lines between financial and technology sectors (Donovan, 2012). For instance, decentralized finance (DeFi) platforms enable peer-to-peer lending, borrowing, and trading without intermediaries, challenging traditional regulatory concepts such as centralization, intermediation, and custody (Macha, 2016). Regulators must grapple with the implications of decentralized technologies for investor protection, market transparency, and systemic stability, while also ensuring compliance with existing legal and regulatory frameworks (Bazot, 2018).

The challenges in regulating fintech within the AU Peace and Security Architecture reflect the complexities and uncertainties inherent in balancing innovation with regulatory oversight and security considerations (Engel, 2014). However, addressing these challenges requires coordinated efforts among AU institutions, regulatory bodies, policymakers, and relevant stakeholders to develop adaptive and forward-looking regulatory frameworks that promote innovation while safeguarding against emerging security risks.

Implementation of Fintech in African Union States

Case Studies of Adoption

Examining case studies of fintech adoption within the African Union (AU) provides valuable insights into the dynamics shaping regulatory frameworks, implementation practices, and security implications across different contexts(Adebajo,2010). One notable case study is the adoption of mobile money platforms in Kenya, particularly the success story of M-Pesa. Launched in 2007 by Safaricom, M-Pesa revolutionized financial services in Kenya by allowing users to send and receive money, pay bills, and access credit using their mobile phones (Arner, 2015). M-Pesa's rapid uptake and widespread adoption transformed Kenya into a global leader in mobile money innovation, with significant implications for financial inclusion and economic development. This case study highlights the role of regulatory innovation, private sector collaboration, and technological innovation in driving fintech adoption and promoting inclusive financial ecosystems (Demir, 2020).

Similarly, the case of Nigeria's fintech industry offers insights into the challenges and opportunities associated with regulatory frameworks and implementation practices (Arner, 2020). Nigeria has emerged as one of Africa's leading fintech hubs, with a vibrant ecosystem of startups and innovation hubs driving financial inclusion and entrepreneurship. However, the regulatory environment in Nigeria presents both opportunities and challenges for fintech firms. While the Central Bank has introduced guidelines for regulating payment service providers and mobile money operators, challenges persist in effectively enforcing regulations and addressing emerging security risks such as cyberattacks and money laundering. This case study underscores the importance of regulatory clarity, enforcement capacity, and collaboration among stakeholders in fostering an enabling environment for fintech innovation (Tchamyou, 2019).

Moreover, the case of South Africa's regulatory sandbox initiative provides insights into the role of experimentation and regulatory innovation in promoting fintech development (Didenko, 2017). The South African Reserve Bank (SARB) launched a regulatory sandbox in 2019 to facilitate the testing of innovative fintech solutions in a controlled environment. This initiative allows fintech firms to experiment with new products and services while regulators monitor their impact and assess potential risks. By providing regulatory certainty and flexibility, the sandbox fosters innovation and entrepreneurship in the fintech sector while managing regulatory risks. This case study highlights the importance of regulatory agility, collaboration, and stakeholder engagement in fostering an inclusive and dynamic fintech ecosystem (Demir, 2020).

Furthermore, the case of Ghana's Payment Systems and Services Act offers insights into the evolving regulatory landscape and its implications for fintech adoption and security (Camilla, 2019). In 2019, Ghana enacted the Payment Systems and Services Act to regulate electronic payments and promote financial inclusion while addressing cybersecurity risks and protecting consumer rights. The Act establishes licensing requirements, operational standards, and cybersecurity protocols for payment service providers, fintech firms, and other stakeholders. By providing regulatory clarity and consumer protection, the Act aims to foster trust and confidence in digital financial services while mitigating security risks. This case study underscores the importance of regulatory certainty, compliance, and collaboration in promoting responsible fintech innovation and safeguarding against security threats (Fuster, 2019).

Socio-economic Factors

Socio-economic factors play a pivotal role in shaping the adoption and impact of fintech within the African Union (AU). Understanding these factors is crucial for policymakers, regulators, and industry stakeholders to effectively promote inclusive and sustainable fintech ecosystems across the continent (Dokken, 2008). One significant socio-economic factor is the level of digital infrastructure and connectivity within a country. Countries with robust telecommunications infrastructure and widespread internet access, such as Kenya and South Africa, have witnessed greater uptake of fintech solutions. For example, Kenya's high mobile penetration rate and widespread use of mobile money platforms like M-Pesa have facilitated financial inclusion and entrepreneurship, particularly in underserved rural areas. In contrast, countries with limited digital infrastructure face challenges in accessing fintech services, hindering adoption and widening the digital divide (Nanziri,2017).

Additionally, socioeconomic factors such as income inequality, poverty levels, and financial literacy influence the demand for fintech services and the ability of individuals to access and use these services effectively (Joshua et al., 2017). In countries with high levels of income inequality, fintech solutions have the potential to bridge the gap by providing affordable and accessible financial services to underserved populations. For instance, in Nigeria, fintech startups like PiggyVest and Flutterwave are leveraging technology to offer savings, investment, and payment solutions to low-income earners and small businesses, empowering them to manage their finances and build wealth. However, challenges remain in addressing barriers to adoption, such as limited digital literacy and trust in fintech platforms, particularly among marginalized communities (Philippon, 2016).

Moreover, regulatory environments and policy frameworks influence the socio-economic dynamics of fintech adoption and usage within the AU context. Countries with clear and supportive regulatory frameworks, such as Ghana and Rwanda, have seen greater fintech innovation and investment, driving economic growth and job creation (Andrianaivo, 2012). For example, Ghana's Payment Systems and Services Act provides a conducive regulatory environment for fintech firms to operate, fostering competition, innovation, and consumer protection. In contrast, countries with restrictive or ambiguous regulations may deter fintech investment and innovation, limiting the potential benefits of fintech for socio-economic development (Fu, 2020).

Furthermore, cultural attitudes and societal norms shape attitudes toward fintech and financial behavior within AU member states (Munlo et al.,2013). For instance, in countries where cash is king and traditional banking services are mistrusted, fintech solutions that offer digital payments and mobile banking may face cultural resistance and adoption barriers. Overcoming cultural barriers requires targeted education and awareness campaigns to build trust and confidence in fintech platforms (Bianchetti, 2018). For example, in Ethiopia, where traditional banking dominates, the government's efforts to promote mobile banking through initiatives like the National Digital Payment Strategy aim to shift cultural attitudes towards digital financial services and foster financial inclusion (Ouma, 2017).

Socio-economic factors significantly influence the adoption, usage, and impact of fintech within the AU context (Glas, 2018). By understanding these factors and addressing associated challenges, stakeholders can develop targeted strategies and interventions to promote inclusive, sustainable, and equitable fintech ecosystems across Africa. From improving digital infrastructure and literacy to fostering supportive regulatory environments and addressing cultural barriers, addressing socio-economic factors is essential for harnessing the transformative potential of fintech to drive economic growth, financial inclusion, and socio-economic development across the continent (Dokken, 2008).

Challenges and Successes

The adoption of fintech within the African Union (AU) presents both challenges and successes that reflect the dynamic nature of the fintech landscape and its impact on the socio-economic fabric of the continent (Abrahamyan, 2019). One significant challenge is the digital divide, which persists across many AU member states due to disparities in digital infrastructure, internet connectivity, and digital literacy. Countries with limited access to digital technologies face barriers to adopting fintech solutions, hindering financial inclusion and economic development. For example, in rural areas where internet connectivity is scarce, accessing fintech services such as mobile banking or digital payments may be challenging, limiting the reach and impact of fintech initiatives (Philippon, 2016).

Moreover, regulatory uncertainty and fragmentation pose challenges for fintech firms operating within the AU context. The lack of clear and consistent regulatory frameworks across AU member states creates compliance burdens and market entry barriers for fintech startups and innovators. For instance, navigating disparate licensing requirements, compliance standards, and regulatory oversight mechanisms can be complex and costly, particularly for startups with limited resources. Regulatory uncertainty also undermines investor confidence and stifles innovation, hindering the growth of the fintech ecosystem (Abor, 2020). However, successes have been observed in countries that have implemented supportive regulatory frameworks conducive to fintech innovation. For example, Ghana's

Payment Systems and Services Act provides a clear regulatory framework for fintech firms, fostering competition, innovation, and consumer protection. Similarly, Kenya's regulatory sandbox initiative allows fintech startups to test innovative solutions in a controlled environment, promoting experimentation and reducing regulatory barriers to entry (Bazot, 2018).

Furthermore, cybersecurity threats and data privacy concerns pose significant challenges to the adoption of fintech within the AU context. The increasing digitization of financial services exposes users to cyberattacks, fraud, and data breaches, undermining trust and confidence in fintech platforms (Demir, 2020). For instance, phishing attacks targeting mobile banking users and ransomware attacks against financial institutions pose risks to the integrity and security of digital financial systems. Moreover, data privacy regulations such as the General Data Protection Regulation (GDPR) in Europe and the Personal Data Protection Act (PDPA) in Singapore present compliance challenges for fintech firms operating in multiple jurisdictions (Manyika, 2016). However, successes have been observed in countries that have implemented robust cybersecurity measures and data protection regulations to mitigate these risks. For example, South Africa's Protection of Personal Information Act (POPIA) sets out comprehensive data protection requirements for fintech firms, safeguarding user privacy and enhancing trust in digital financial services (Ahmad, 2019).

Additionally, financial literacy and consumer education are essential for ensuring the responsible adoption and usage of fintech within the AU context. Many users, particularly those in underserved communities, lack the necessary knowledge and skills to make informed financial decisions and protect themselves from financial risks (Nanziri,2017). For instance, understanding the terms and conditions of digital financial services, managing digital identities, and recognizing phishing attempts are critical skills for safeguarding against fraud and exploitation. However, successes have been observed in countries that have implemented financial literacy programs and consumer education initiatives to empower users with the knowledge and skills to navigate the digital financial landscape responsibly. For example, Kenya's M-Pesa platform provides users with educational materials and training workshops to promote financial literacy and empower them to make informed financial decisions (Burns,2016).

The adoption of fintech within the AU context presents a range of challenges and successes that reflect the complexities and opportunities inherent in the fintech landscape(Gardachew,2020). By addressing challenges related to digital infrastructure, regulatory uncertainty, cybersecurity threats, and financial literacy, stakeholders can unlock the transformative potential of fintech to drive inclusive economic growth, financial inclusion, and socio-economic development across Africa. Through targeted interventions and collaborative efforts, the AU and its member states can overcome these challenges and capitalize on the successes to build resilient, inclusive, and sustainable fintech ecosystems that benefit all stakeholders.

Security Implications of Fintech

Cybersecurity Threats

Cybersecurity threats within the African Peace and Security Architecture represent a critical challenge for the continent's stability and development (Badejo,2008). As digital technologies continue to permeate various sectors, including finance, healthcare, and governance, the risk of cyberattacks targeting critical infrastructure, sensitive data, and essential services has increased (Arner, 2015). These threats not only undermine the integrity and security of digital systems but also pose significant risks to peace and security, economic stability, and public trust. One example of cybersecurity threats within the African Peace and Security Architecture is the proliferation of ransomware attacks targeting government agencies, financial institutions, and healthcare providers. Ransomware attacks involve malicious actors encrypting critical data and demanding ransom payments in exchange for decryption keys, disrupting operations and causing financial losses (Beck, 2013). For instance, in 2017, the WannaCry ransomware attack affected thousands of computers worldwide, including those in African countries such as Nigeria and South Africa, highlighting the global reach and impact of cyber threats (Bianchetti, 2018).

Furthermore, phishing attacks targeting individuals, businesses, and government agencies pose significant cybersecurity risks within the African Peace and Security Architecture (Gumedze, 2011). Phishing attacks involve deceptive emails, messages, or websites designed to trick users into disclosing sensitive information such as passwords, financial credentials, or personal data. These attacks can lead to identity theft, financial fraud, and unauthorized access to confidential information, compromising national security and public trust. For example, in 2020, the South African Revenue Service (SARS) issued warnings about phishing scams targeting taxpayers, urging vigilance and caution when handling electronic communications. Similarly, government agencies and financial institutions across Africa have reported phishing attacks aimed at stealing sensitive information and conducting fraudulent activities, highlighting the pervasive nature of this cybersecurity threat (Fu, 2020).

Moreover, the rise of cyber espionage and state-sponsored attacks poses significant challenges to the African Union (Joshua et al., 2017). State actors, including foreign governments and cybercriminal groups, engage in cyber espionage activities to gather intelligence, disrupt operations, and undermine national security (Kang, 2016). These attacks target government agencies, defense organizations, and critical infrastructure sectors such as energy, telecommunications, and transportation, posing risks to national sovereignty and regional stability (Arner, 2015). For example, in 2019, the African Union experienced a cybersecurity breach that compromised confidential data and sensitive communications, raising concerns about the vulnerability of pan-African institutions to cyber threats (Ouma, 2017). Similarly, reports of state-sponsored cyberattacks targeting African governments and organizations underscore the need for enhanced cybersecurity measures and cooperation among AU member states to defend against emerging threats effectively.

Cybersecurity threats within the African Peace and Security Architecture represent a multifaceted challenge that requires coordinated efforts and strategic responses to mitigate risks and enhance resilience (Engel, 2014). By strengthening cybersecurity capabilities, raising awareness, and promoting collaboration among governments, private sector entities, and civil society organizations, stakeholders can address the evolving nature of cyber threats and safeguard Africa's peace, security, and prosperity (Didenko, 2017). Moreover, investing in cybersecurity infrastructure, capacity building, and information-sharing mechanisms is essential for building a resilient cybersecurity ecosystem that can withstand emerging threats and protect critical digital assets and systems (Salami, 2019). Through proactive measures and collective action, the AU and its member states can effectively address cybersecurity threats and ensure the integrity and security of digital systems within the African continent.

Financial Risks

Financial risks represent a significant concern within the African Peace and Security Architecture, posing threats to economic stability, public trust, and socio-political cohesion(Gumedze, 2011). These risks encompass a range of factors, including fraud, money laundering, corruption, and illicit financial flows, which undermine the integrity and resilience of financial systems and institutions. One example of financial risks within the African Peace and Security Architecture is the prevalence of corruption and embezzlement, which siphons off public funds and undermines the effectiveness of government institutions and services. Corruption erodes public trust in governance, fosters inequality, and perpetuates cycles of poverty and instability, posing systemic risks to peace and security. For instance, the mismanagement of public finances and the diversion of funds intended for development projects contribute to social unrest, political instability, and conflict in countries across Africa (Tchamyou, 2019).

Furthermore, money laundering represents a significant financial risk within the African Peace and Security Architecture, enabling criminal organizations to launder illicit proceeds and finance illicit activities such as terrorism, drug trafficking, and human trafficking (Andrianaivo, 2012). Money laundering involves disguising the origins of illicit funds through a series of complex financial transactions, making it difficult for authorities to trace and disrupt illicit financial flows. For example, in 2019, the Financial Action Task Force (FATF) identified several African countries, including Nigeria, South Africa, and Kenya, as high-risk jurisdictions for money laundering and terrorist financing, highlighting the pervasive nature of this financial risk. Moreover, weak regulatory frameworks, inadequate enforcement capacity, and porous borders exacerbate money laundering risks, undermining efforts to combat financial crime and ensure financial integrity within the African continent (Camilla, 2019).

Additionally, the proliferation of fraudulent schemes and financial scams poses significant financial risks within the African Peace and Security Architecture, targeting individuals, businesses, and government agencies. These schemes, which include Ponzi schemes, pyramid schemes, and investment fraud, exploit vulnerabilities in financial systems and prey on unsuspecting victims, causing financial losses and eroding trust in financial institutions (Bazot, 2018). For instance, in 2020, the collapse of several Ponzi schemes in Nigeria, such as MMM Nigeria and Racksterli, led to widespread financial losses and public outcry, highlighting the risks associated with fraudulent investment schemes (Sy, 2019).

Moreover, the rise of digital financial services and fintech platforms has created new opportunities for fraudsters to perpetrate scams and financial crimes, posing challenges for regulators and law enforcement agencies to detect and prevent fraudulent activities effectively (Makina,2019).

Financial risks within the African Peace and Security Architecture represent complex and interconnected challenges that require coordinated efforts and strategic responses to mitigate risks and enhance resilience (Stewart et al., 2018). By strengthening regulatory frameworks, enhancing enforcement capacity, and promoting transparency and accountability in financial systems, stakeholders can address the root causes of financial risks and safeguard Africa's economic stability, public trust, and socio-political cohesion (Bianchetti, 2018). Moreover, investing in financial literacy, consumer education, and anti-corruption measures is essential for building a resilient financial ecosystem that can withstand emerging threats and promote sustainable development across the continent.

Impact on Security Dynamics

The impact of financial technology (fintech) on security dynamics within the African Peace and Security Architecture is multifaceted, influencing various aspects of security, including economic stability, cybersecurity, and transnational crime (Joshua et al., 2017). Fintech innovations have the potential to disrupt traditional financial systems and alter security dynamics in profound ways, presenting both opportunities and challenges for peace and stability across the continent. One significant impact of fintech on security dynamics is its role in promoting economic inclusion and resilience (Donovan, 2012). By expanding access to financial services and empowering underserved populations, fintech fosters economic empowerment, reduces inequality, and enhances socio-economic stability (Aker, 2010). For example, mobile money platforms like M-Pesa in Kenya and Paga in Nigeria have transformed the financial landscape, enabling millions of individuals to access banking services, transfer money, and access credit, thereby contributing to poverty reduction and economic development (Makina,2019).

However, the widespread adoption of fintech also introduces new security risks and vulnerabilities that can undermine peace and security within the African continent (Demirgüç-Kunt, 2018). One such risk is the proliferation of cyber threats targeting digital financial systems, including phishing attacks, malware infections, and data breaches. The increasing digitization of financial transactions and the reliance on digital platforms make fintech ecosystems attractive targets for cybercriminals seeking to exploit vulnerabilities and steal sensitive information. For instance, cyberattacks targeting financial institutions and payment systems can disrupt economic activities, erode public trust, and undermine confidence in digital financial services, posing systemic risks to economic stability and security (Ouma, 2017).

Moreover, the anonymity and borderless nature of fintech transactions facilitate illicit financial activities such as money laundering, terrorist financing, and transnational crime, posing challenges for law enforcement agencies and security institutions within the African Peace and Security Architecture (Buchak, 2018). Criminal organizations and terrorist groups exploit fintech platforms to launder illicit proceeds, finance illegal activities, and evade detection, undermining efforts to combat financial crime and ensure financial integrity. For example, the use of cryptocurrencies and decentralized finance (DeFi) platforms enables criminals to conduct anonymous and untraceable transactions, complicating efforts to track and disrupt illicit financial flows (Philippon, 2016).

Furthermore, the intersection of fintech with emerging security threats, such as hybrid warfare, disinformation campaigns, and cyber warfare, poses complex challenges for security institutions and policymakers within the African continent (Didenko, 2017). State actors and non-state actors increasingly leverage digital technologies and social media platforms to influence public opinion, spread propaganda, and manipulate information, exacerbating social tensions, political instability, and conflict dynamics. For instance, the use of social media platforms to incite violence, disseminate hate speech, and spread extremist ideologies poses risks to social cohesion and undermines efforts to build peace and reconciliation in conflict-affected areas.

The impact of fintech on security dynamics within the African Peace and Security Architecture is profound and multifaceted, presenting both opportunities and challenges for peace and stability across the continent. While fintech innovations have the potential to promote economic inclusion and resilience, they also introduce new security risks and vulnerabilities that require proactive and coordinated responses from policymakers, regulators, and security institutions (Beck, 2013). By addressing these challenges and harnessing the transformative potential of fintech for peace and security, stakeholders can build resilient and inclusive fintech ecosystems that contribute to sustainable development and prosperity in Africa (Demir, 2020).

Policy Recommendations

Strengthening Fintech Regulations and Oversight Mechanisms

Strengthening fintech regulations and oversight mechanisms within the African Union (AU) and the African Union Peace and Security Architecture is crucial for promoting financial stability, consumer protection, and cybersecurity resilience across the continent. One key aspect of strengthening regulations is enhancing regulatory clarity and coherence to provide a conducive environment for fintech innovation while safeguarding against emerging risks. For example, the AU could work towards harmonizing regulatory frameworks across member states to ensure consistency in licensing requirements, compliance standards, and oversight mechanisms. By establishing common regulatory principles and guidelines, the AU can streamline the regulatory process and reduce compliance burdens for fintech firms operating in multiple jurisdictions, fostering cross-border innovation and investment.

Moreover, strengthening oversight mechanisms is essential for monitoring and enforcing compliance with FinTech regulations and addressing emerging risks effectively. The AU could establish mechanisms for coordinating regulatory supervision and information sharing among national regulators, regional bodies, and international organizations to enhance regulatory effectiveness and responsiveness. For instance, the AU could create a pan-African regulatory body or task force dedicated to overseeing fintech developments and addressing cross-border regulatory challenges. By fostering collaboration and coordination among stakeholders, such as financial regulators, law enforcement agencies, and industry associations, the AU can strengthen oversight mechanisms and promote regulatory convergence within the African fintech ecosystem.

Furthermore, capacity building and technical assistance initiatives play a critical role in strengthening fintech regulations and oversight mechanisms within the AU and the African Peace and Security Architecture. The AU could support capacity-building programs and training workshops for regulators, policymakers, and industry stakeholders to enhance their understanding of fintech developments, regulatory best practices, and cybersecurity risks. For example, the AU could collaborate with international partners, such as the World Bank and the International Monetary Fund (IMF), to provide technical assistance and knowledge-sharing opportunities for AU member states. By investing in human capital and institutional capacity, the AU can strengthen regulatory capacity and resilience, enabling regulators to adapt to evolving fintech trends and address emerging security challenges effectively.

Additionally, promoting public-private partnerships and stakeholder engagement is essential for fostering trust, transparency, and accountability in fintech regulations and oversight mechanisms within the AU. The AU could convene multi-stakeholder forums and consultations to facilitate dialogue and collaboration among governments, financial institutions, fintech firms, civil society organizations, and academia. By involving diverse stakeholders in the policymaking process, the AU can ensure that regulatory frameworks and oversight mechanisms reflect the needs and priorities of all stakeholders, fostering consensus-building and stakeholder buy-in. For example, the AU could establish advisory committees or working groups comprising representatives from the public and private sectors to provide input and feedback on fintech regulations and policies.

Strengthening fintech regulations and oversight mechanisms within the African Union and the African Union Peace and Security Architecture is essential for promoting financial stability, consumer protection, and cybersecurity resilience across the continent. By enhancing regulatory clarity, coherence, and effectiveness, investing in capacity building and technical assistance, and promoting stakeholder engagement and collaboration, the AU can create an enabling environment for responsible fintech innovation that contributes to peace, security, and prosperity in Africa. Through concerted efforts and collective action, stakeholders can address emerging challenges and harness the transformative potential of fintech to drive inclusive and sustainable development across the continent.

Enhancing Cybersecurity Measures

Enhancing cybersecurity measures within the African Union (AU) and the African Union Peace and Security Architecture is imperative to mitigate the evolving threats posed by cyberattacks and safeguard critical digital infrastructure and systems. One crucial aspect of enhancing cybersecurity measures is the development and implementation of comprehensive cybersecurity frameworks and strategies tailored to the specific needs and challenges of AU member states. For example, the AU could collaborate with regional organizations such as the Economic Community of West African States (ECOWAS) and the Southern African Development Community (SADC) to develop regional cybersecurity frameworks that align with international best practices and standards. These frameworks could outline key cybersecurity principles, guidelines for risk management, incident response protocols, and capacity-building initiatives to enhance cybersecurity resilience across the continent.

Furthermore, investing in cybersecurity capacity building and technical assistance is essential for strengthening the AU's cybersecurity capabilities and fostering a culture of cybersecurity awareness and resilience. The AU could support capacity-building programs and training workshops for government officials, law enforcement agencies, and cybersecurity professionals to enhance their technical skills and knowledge of cybersecurity threats and best practices. For example, the AU could collaborate with international partners such as the United Nations Office on Drugs and Crime (UNODC) and the International Telecommunication Union (ITU) to deliver cybersecurity training and certification programs for AU member states. By investing in human capital and institutional capacity, the AU can enhance its ability to detect, prevent, and respond to cyber threats effectively.

Moreover, promoting information sharing and collaboration among AU member states, regional organizations, and international partners is essential for enhancing cybersecurity resilience and combating cyber threats effectively. The AU could establish a cybersecurity information-sharing platform or network to facilitate the exchange of threat intelligence, best practices, and lessons learned among stakeholders. For example, the AU could leverage existing platforms such as the Africa Cybersecurity and Data Protection Forum (ACDPF) to promote collaboration and coordination on cybersecurity issues. By fostering a culture of information sharing and collaboration, the AU can enhance situational awareness, strengthen collective defense capabilities, and respond more effectively to cyber threats and incidents across the continent.

Additionally, strengthening legal and regulatory frameworks is essential for addressing gaps in cybersecurity governance and promoting compliance with cybersecurity standards and norms within the AU and its member states. The AU could work with member states to develop and implement cybersecurity laws, regulations, and policies that align with international best practices and promote accountability and transparency. For example, the AU could support the adoption of national cybersecurity strategies that outline priorities, objectives, and action plans for enhancing cybersecurity resilience and protecting critical infrastructure. By providing guidance and technical assistance, the AU can help member states strengthen their legal and regulatory frameworks and promote a coordinated and harmonized approach to cybersecurity governance across the continent.

Enhancing cybersecurity measures within the African Union and the African Union Peace and Security Architecture is essential for addressing evolving cyber threats and protecting critical digital infrastructure and systems across the continent. By developing comprehensive cybersecurity frameworks, investing in capacity building and technical assistance, promoting information sharing and collaboration, and strengthening legal and regulatory frameworks, the AU can enhance its cybersecurity resilience and contribute to a safer and more secure cyberspace for all Africans. Through concerted efforts and collective action, stakeholders can build a resilient cybersecurity ecosystem that effectively addresses emerging threats and promotes peace, stability, and prosperity in Africa.

Promoting Collaboration and Information Sharing

Promoting collaboration and information sharing within the African Union (AU) and the African Union Peace and Security Architecture is essential for addressing cybersecurity threats effectively and building resilience against emerging risks. Collaboration among AU member states, regional organizations, international partners, and the private sector is crucial for enhancing situational awareness, sharing threat intelligence, and coordinating responses to cyber incidents. One example of successful collaboration is the AU's partnership with the African Telecommunications Union (ATU) to establish the Africa Cybersecurity and Data Protection Forum (ACDPF). This platform facilitates dialogue, cooperation, and information sharing among African countries on cybersecurity issues, enabling stakeholders to exchange best practices, lessons learned, and technical expertise.

Moreover, promoting collaboration and information sharing among AU member states and regional organizations fosters a collective defense approach to cybersecurity, where countries work together to detect, prevent, and respond to cyber threats collectively. For example, the East African Community (EAC) has established a regional cybersecurity center to promote collaboration among member states in addressing cyber threats and building cybersecurity capacity.

This center serves as a focal point for coordinating cybersecurity activities, sharing threat intelligence, and providing technical assistance and training to member states, enhancing regional cybersecurity resilience and cooperation.

Furthermore, promoting collaboration and information sharing between the public and private sectors is essential for strengthening cybersecurity resilience and addressing emerging threats effectively. The AU could establish public-private partnerships and industry forums to facilitate dialogue, cooperation, and information sharing between governments, businesses, and technology providers. For example, the AU could collaborate with leading technology companies and financial institutions to establish a cybersecurity information-sharing platform or threat intelligence-sharing consortium. By fostering trust and collaboration between public and private stakeholders, the AU can enhance its ability to detect, prevent, and respond to cyber threats, leveraging the expertise and resources of the private sector to strengthen cybersecurity resilience across the continent.

Additionally, promoting collaboration and information sharing at the international level is essential for addressing transnational cyber threats and promoting global cybersecurity cooperation. The AU could strengthen partnerships with international organizations, such as the United Nations, the African Union, and the International Telecommunication Union (ITU), to promote cybersecurity capacity building, technical assistance, and information-sharing initiatives. For example, the AU could collaborate with the ITU's Global Cybersecurity Agenda (GCA) to develop regional cybersecurity capacity-building programs and establish regional cybersecurity centers of excellence. By leveraging international partnerships and resources, the AU can enhance its cybersecurity resilience contribute to global efforts to combat cyber threats, and promote a safer and more secure cyberspace for all.

Promoting collaboration and information sharing within the African Union and the African Union Peace and Security Architecture is essential for building resilience against cyber threats and promoting cybersecurity cooperation across the continent. By fostering collaboration among AU member states, regional organizations, international partners, and the private sector, stakeholders can enhance situational awareness, share threat intelligence, and coordinate responses to cyber incidents effectively. Through concerted efforts and collective action, the AU can strengthen its cybersecurity resilience and contribute to a safer and more secure cyberspace for all Africans.

References

Abor, J. Y. (2020). Exploring the impact of the COVID-19 pandemic on the FinTech space in Africa (Working Paper Series No. 7/2020, Center for Global Finance, SOAS University of London). https://www.centreforglobalfinance.org/2020-working-papers

Abor, J.Y., Issahaku, H., Amidu, M. and Murinde, V. (2020). Financial inclusion and economic growth. In J. Y. Abor, C. K. D. Adjasi, & R. Lensink (Eds.), Contemporary issues in development finance (p. 263).

Abor, J. Y., Amidu, M. and Issahaku, H. (2018). Mobile telephony, financial inclusion, and inclusive growth. Journal of African Affairs, 19(3), 430-453.

Abrahamyan, Mira. (December 1, 2019). "Tony Karbo and Kudrat Virk (eds.): The Palgrave Handbook of Peacebuilding in Africa." Czech Journal of International Relations 54, no. 4: 81–84. http://dx.doi.org/10.32422/mv.1654.

Adebajo, Adekeye. (2010). The curse of Berlin: Africa after the Cold War. New York: Columbia University Press.

AFI. (2017, July). Define financial inclusion. afi-global.org.https://www.afi-global.org/sites/default/files/publications/2017-07/FIS_GN_28_AW_digital.pdf

AFI. (September 4, 2018). FinTech for Financial Inclusion: A Framework for Digital Financial Transformation. afi-global.org. https://www.afi-global.org/publications/fintechforfinancialinclusionaframework-for-digital-financial-transformation/

Afrikstart. (2016, September). Crowdfunding in Africa. afrikstart.com. http://afrikstart.com/report/wpcontent/uploads/2016/09/AfrikstartCrowdfunding-In-Africa-Report.pdf

Ahmad, A.H., Green, C., & Jiang, F. (2020). Mobile money, financial inclusion, and development: a review of the African experience. Journal of Economic Studies, 34(4), 753-792.

Ahmad, E., Dowling, D., Chan, D., Colenbrander, S. and Godfrey, N. (April 2019). Increasing investments for sustainable urban infrastructure: a guide for national and subnational reforms. The report, Global Commission on the Economy and Climate.

Aker, J.C. and Mbiti, I.M. (2010). Mobile phones and economic development in Africa. Journal of Economic Perspectives, 24(3), 207-232.

Allen, F., Demirguc-Kunt, A., Klapper, L. and Peria, MSM (2016). The foundations of financial inclusion: Understanding the ownership and use of formal accounts. Journal of Financial Intermediation, 27, 1–30.

Alt, R., Eckert, C. and Puschmann, T. (2015). Network and service management systems: the case of German and Swiss banks. Information Resource Management Journal (IRMJ), 28(1), 38-56.

Amadou N., R. Maino, A. Massara, H. Perez Saiz and P. Sharma. FinTech in sub-Saharan African countries: a game changer? International Monetary Fund.

Amidu, M., Abor, J. Y. and Issahaku, H. (2018). Inclusive finance, financial literacy, and household livelihood activities in Ghana. Center for Global Finance.

Andrianaivo, M. and Kpodar, K. (2012). Mobile phones, financial inclusion, and growth. Review of Economics and Institutions, 3(2), 30.

Arner, DW, Zetzsche, DA, Buckley, RP, & Barberis, JN (2017). FinTech and RegTech: Enabling innovation while preserving financial stability. Georgetown Journal of International Affairs, 47-58.

Arner, D.W., Barberis, J., & Buckley, R.P. (2015). The evolution of Fintech: a new post-crisis paradigm. Georgetown Journal of International Law, 47, 1271.

Arner, DW, Barberis, JN, Walker, J., Buckley, RP, Dahdal, AM, & Zetzsche, DA (2020). Digital finance and the COVID-19 crisis (University of Hong Kong Faculty of Law Research Paper 2020/017).

Aron, J. (2018). Mobile money and the economy: a review of the evidence. The World Bank Research Observer, 33(2), 135-188.

Badejo, Diedre. (2008). The African Union. New York: Chelsea House.

Banya, R. M. and Biekpe, N. (2017). Banking competition and economic growth: Empirical evidence from selected African border countries. Journal of Economic Studies, 44(2), 245-265.

Bazot, G. (2018). Financial consumption and the cost of financing: measuring financial efficiency in Europe (1950-2007). Journal of the European Economic Association, 16(1), 123-160.

Beck, T., and Cull. R. (2013). The Banking Sector in Africa (World Bank Policy Research Working Paper 6684).

Bianchetti, M., Ricci, C. and Scaringi, M. (2018). Are cryptocurrencies real financial bubbles? Evidence from quantitative analyses. Evidence from quantitative analyzes (February 24, 2018). A version of this article was published in Risk 26.

Buchak, G., Matvos, G., Piskorski, T., and Seru, A. (2018). Fintech, regulatory arbitrage and the rise of shadow banks. Journal of Financial Economics, 130(3), 453-483.

Burns, S. (2016). Finance for All: The Success of the Market-Driven Financial Development Approach in Developing Countries (AIER Sound Money Project Working Paper forthcoming).

Camilla, N. (2019). Decentralized monetary systems. Available at SSRN 3498841.

Demir, A., Pesqué-Quand, V., Altunbas, Y. and Murinde, V. (2020) Fintech, financial inclusion and income inequality: a quantile regression approach. The European Journal of Finance, 1–22.

Demirgüç-Kunt, A. and Levine, R. (2018). Finance and growth. Edward Elgar Publishing Limited.

Demirguc-Kunt, A., Klapper, L., Singer, D., Ansar, S., and Hess, J. (2018). The Global Findex 2017 Database: Measuring Financial Inclusion and the Fintech Revolution. The World Bank.

Demirgüç-Kunt, A., Honohan, P. and Beck, T. (2008). Finance for all? : Policies and pitfalls related to expanding access. The World Bank.

Didenko, A. (2017). Regulating FinTech: lessons from Africa. San Diego Journal of International Law, 19, 311.

Dokken, Karin. (2008). "The Security Politics of the African Union." In African Security Politics Redefined, 119–46. New York: Palgrave Macmillan US, http://dx.doi.org/10.1057/9780230612495_5.

Doku, JN, Abor, J., Adjasi, CKD and Andoh, C. (2012). Assessing competitive behavior in the emerging banking market: African evidence. In Finance and Development in Africa. Emerald Group Publishing Limited.

Donovan, K. (2012). Mobile money for financial inclusion. Information and Communication for Development, 61(1), 61-73.

El Abdellaoui, Jamila.(2010) "The African Union and Security in Africa." In New Security Threats and Crises in Africa, 19–38. New York: Palgrave Macmillan US. http://dx.doi.org/10.1057/9780230115538_2.

Engel, Ulf. (July 3, 2014)."The African Union, the African Peace and Security Architecture, and Maritime Security." African Security 7, no. 3: 207–27. http://dx.doi.org/10.1080/19392206.2014.939889.

Financial Action Task Force. (October 19, 2018). Regulation of virtual assets. fatf-gafi.org.https://www.fatfgafi.org/publications/fatfrecommendations/documents/regulation-virtual-assets.html

Financial Action Task Force. (2015, June). Virtual currencies: tips for a risk-based approach.fatfgafi.org.https://www.fatfgafi.org/media/fatf/documents/reports/Guidance-RBA-Virtual-Currencies.pdf

Financial Stability Board. (June 27, 2017). Implications of FinTech for financial stability: Supervisory and regulatory issues that deserve attention from authorities. fsb.org. https://www.fsb.org/wp-content/uploads/R270617.pdf

Fioramonti, L. (2017). Welfare economics. Pan Macmillan.

Fosu, S. (2013). Banking competition in Africa: sub-regional comparative studies. Emerging Markets Review, 15, 233-254.

Frost, J. (2020). The economic forces driving Fintech adoption in countries. In The Technology Revolution in Financial Services: How Banks, FinTech, and Customers Win Together (p. 70).

Fu, J. and Mishra, M. (2020). The global impact of COVID-19 on Fintech adoption (Swiss Finance Institute Research Paper 20-38).

Fuster, A., Plosser, M., Schnabl, P., and Vickery, J. (2019). The role of technology in mortgage lending. The review of financial studies, 32(5), 1854-1899.

Gardachew, Bewuketu D. (December 15, 2020). "The African Peace and Security Architecture as a Tool for the Maintenance of Peace and Security. Part 1." RUDN Journal of Public Administration 7, no. 3: 179–94. http://dx.doi.org/10.22363/2312-8313-2020-7-3-179-194.

Glas, Aarie. (September 1, 2018). "African Union security culture in practice: African problems and African solutions." International Affairs 94, no. 5: 1121–38. http://dx.doi.org/10.1093/ia/iiy116.

Gumedze, Sabelo. (2011). The Peace and Security Council of the African Union: Its relationship with the United Nations, the African Union and sub-regional mechanisms. Åbo: Åbo Akademi University Press.

Gosavi, A. (2018). Can mobile money help businesses alleviate the access to finance challenge in Eastern Sub-Saharan Africa? Journal of African Affairs, 19(3), 343-360.

GPFI. (2016a, July 24). G20 High-Level Principles for Digital Financial Inclusion.gpfi.org.https://www.gpfi.org/sites/gpfi/files/documents/G20%20High%20Level%20Principles%20for%20Digital%20Financial%20Inclusion%20-%20Full%20version-.pdf

GSMA. (2018, May). Report on the state of the mobile money industry. gsma.com.https://www.gsma.com/mobilefordevelopment/wpcontent/uploads/2018/05/GSMA_2017State_of_the_Industry_Report_on_Mobile_Money_Full_Report.pdf

GSMA. (2019). Report on the state of the mobile money industry. https://www.gsma.com/sotir/wp-content/uploads/2020/03/GSMA-State-of-the-Industry-Report-on-Mobile-Money-2019-Full-Report.pdf

GSMA. (2020, March). Report on the state of the mobile money industry. gsma.com. https://www.gsma.com/sotir/wp-content/uploads/2020/03/GSMA-State-of-the-Industry-Report-on-Mobile-Money-2019-Full-Report.pdf

Hammed, Hanafi A. (December 1, 2015). "Appraising the Role of African Union: the New Partnership for Africa's Development in Conflict Prevention and Management in Africa." International and Comparative Law Review 15, no. 2: 69–88. http://dx.doi.org/10.1515/iclr-2016-0036.

He, Dong., Leckow, RB, Haksar, V., Griffoli, TM, Jenkinson, N., Kashima, M., Khiaorong, T., Rochon, C. and Tourpe, H. (2017). Fintech and Financial Services: Initial Considerations (IMF Staff Discussion Note SDN/17/05).

Jack, W. and Suri, T. (2011). Mobile Money: The Economy of M-PESA (No. w16721. National Bureau of Economic Research).

Jenik, I., Lyman, T., and Nava, A. (2017). Crowdfunding and Financial Inclusion (CGAP [Consultative Group on Assistance to the Poor] Working Paper 41).

Joshua, Segun, and Faith Olanrewaju. (November 1, 2017). "The AU's Progress and Achievements in the Realm of Peace and Security." India Quarterly: A Journal of International Affairs 73, no. 4: 454–71. http://dx.doi.org/10.1177/0974928417731639.

Kang, MS, Back, SJ, & Lim, JI (2016). A study of a self-checklist for personal information protection of FinTech service: For simple payment service. Journal of the Society for Electronic Commerce Studies, 20(4).

Kulhanek, O. (2019). The five rules of data monetization. KPMG. https://home.kpmg/xx/en/home/insights/2019/04/the-five-rules-of-data-monetization.html

Lee, I. and Shin, Y.J. (2018). Fintech: ecosystem, business models, investment decisions and challenges. Business Horizons, 61(1), 35-46.

Makina, D. (2019). The potential of FinTech to enable financial inclusion. In Expanding Financial Inclusion in Africa (pp. 299-318). Academic press.

Manyika, J., Lund, S., Singer, M., White, O., Berry, C. (2016). Digital finance for all: fostering inclusive growth in emerging economies. McKinsey Global Institute, 1-15.

Macha, I. (2016). Macroeconomic Impact of Mobile Payment Services – A Survey of Research Evidence. As part of the International Growth Centre/London School of Economics regional workshop, Freetown, Sierra Leone.

Masssolution. (2013). 2013 CF Crowdfunding Industry Report. compromisoempresarial.com.https://www.compromisoempresarial.com/wpcontent/uploads/137356857-Massolution-2013CF-Excerpt-Revised-04182.pdf

Mbiti, I. and Weil, DN (2016). 7. Mobile Banking: The Impact of M-Pesa in Kenya. University of Chicago Press.

McMillan, J. (January 20, 2015). Banking in the digital age: the failure of financial regulation. theguardian.com. https://www.theguardian.com/sustainablebusiness/2015/jan/20/financeindigitalage-while-regulation-stuck-in-industrial

Morawczynski, O. (2009). Exploring the use and impact of "transformational" mobile financial services: the case of M-PESA in Kenya. Journal of East African Studies, 3(3), 509-525.

Morse, A. (2015). Peer-to-peer crowdfunding: Insights and potential for disruption in consumer lending. Annual Review of Financial Economics, 7, 463-482.

Munlo, I. G., and Brooke A. Smith-Windsor. (2013). AU-NATO collaboration: Implications and prospects. Rome: NATO Defense College, Research Division.

Nanziri, E. L. (2017). Financial inclusion and social protection in post-apartheid South Africa. African Economic Research Consortium.

Ouma, SA, Odongo, TM and Were, M. (2017). Mobile financial services and financial inclusion: is this a boon for mobilizing savings? Development Finance Review, 7(1), 29-35.

Philippon, T. (2016). The Fintech opportunity. No. w22476. National Bureau of Economic Research.

Salami, I. (2019). Alternative financing approaches and regulation in Africa. In Expanding Financial Inclusion in Africa (pp. 279-297). Academic press.

Skan, J., Dickerson, J. and Gagliardi, L. (January 15, 2016). Fintech and the Changing Landscape: Landing Points for the Industry. Accenture. https://www.accenture.com/t20160427T053810__w__/us-en/_acnmedia/PDF-15/Accenture-Fintech-Evolving-Landscape.pdf.

Solf, Ali M. O. (2014). "Managing intra-state conflicts in Africa: the African Union as an effective security actor." Thesis, University of Glasgow. http://theses.gla.ac.uk/5977/.

South African Reserve Bank. (2014). Position paper on virtual currencies (Position Paper Number 02).

Stewart, Colin, and Line Holmung Andersen. (2018) "Partnering for Peace: United Nations and African Union Cooperation in Peace and Security." In African Foreign Policies in International Institutions, 165–81. New York: Palgrave Macmillan US. http://dx.doi.org/10.1057/978-1-137-57574-6_11.

Sy, AN, Maino, R., Massara, A., Saiz, HP, and Sharma, P. (2019). FinTech in sub-Saharan African countries: a game changer? International Monetary Fund.

Tchamyou, VS, Erreygers, G. and Cassimon, D. (2019). Inequalities, ICT and financial access in Africa. Technological Forecasting and Social Change, 139, 169-184.

Quartey, P. (2020). Financial Sector Landscape in Ghana: Background Paper, Global Finance Programme.

Wood, J. C. (2012). "Defining the role of the African Union Peace and Architecture (APSA) : a reconceptualization of the roles of institutions." Thesis, Coventry University. http://curve.coventry.ac.uk/open/items/c211face-e5d4-40ae-bb90-d41d0dff935d/1

World Bank. (October 24, 2013). The potential of crowdfunding for developing countries. infodev.org. https://www.infodev.org/crowdfunding

World Bank. (January 1, 2015). Crowdfunding in Emerging Markets: Lessons from East African Startups. worldbank.org. https://documents.worldbank.org/en/publication/documentsreports/documentdetail/820101468186856874

www.ingramcontent.com/pod-product-compliance
Lightning Source LLC
LaVergne TN
LVHW022044200926
848481LV00003B/773